Interaction in the Thai Bureaucracy

Westview Replica Editions

Interaction in the Thai Bureaucracy:
Structure, Culture, and Social Exchange

David F. Haas

Presenting the results of seventeen months of field research, conducted entirely in the Thai language, this study
describes and compares the patterns of social exchange of two
groups of Thai officials: district-level bureaucrats and
physicians in a provincial hospital. Dr. Haas uses a unique
combination of anthropological field data and survey research.
He is the first to thoroughly describe the effects of the
government's counterinsurgency efforts on the behavior of
local officials and on their relations with villagers and provincial merchants; his chapters on physicians contain one of
the few published discussions of the meaning of professionalism in non-Western societies, as well as the only field study
available of an Asian medical institution.

David F. Haas is assistant professor of sociology and
rural sociology at Louisiana State University.

To my parents

Interaction in the Thai Bureaucracy: Structure, Culture, and Social Exchange

David F. Haas

Westview Press **/** Boulder, Colorado

A Westview Replica Edition

Published in 1979 in the United States of America by
        Westview Press, Inc.
        5500 Central Avenue
        Boulder, Colorado 80301
        Frederick A. Praeger, Publisher

Library of Congress Catalog Card Number: 79-5168
ISBN: 0-89158-578-8

Printed and bound in the United States of America

Contents

Tables and Figures

Figures

Acknowledgments

No substantial research project could be carried out by one person alone, especially when, like this one, it was a maiden effort. I am indebted to many more people than I can list here, but some deserve special mention because of the large roles they have played. First, my teachers in the Department of Sociology of the University of Wisconsin, including my advisor Professor William H. Sewell and Professors David Mechanic and Joseph Elder, made my career as a graduate student both stimulating and enjoyable. They have guided this research from its inception and provided advice, criticism, and encouragement in both theoretical and practical matters at every stage of its development. Without their support this project could never have been carried out. I owe a special debt to Professor Elaine Walster whose warm support, incisive criticism, and theoretical insight have played a large part in my intellectual development. I am also grateful to Professor Daryl J. Hobbs of the Department of Sociology of the University of Missouri. His exciting teaching and personal encouragement brought me into the field of sociology, and I have since come to see my encounter with him as a very lucky moment in my life.

I am also indebted to many people in Thailand who gave generously of their time to help with my research. Unfortunately, the demands of anonymity preclude my thanking publicly each of the officials who submitted to my presence, answered my many questions, and made my stay in their country a pleasure. However, they know who they are, and to them I express my gratitude. The staff of the Research Center at the National Institute of Development Administration gave generous assistance in writing the questionnaire for the second phase of this research. In this connection, I would like to thank especially my research assistant Mr. Prasert Rakthaidi who patiently went over with me each question to assure its correctness both in meaning and usage. Dr. Titaya Suvanajata, the director of the Research Center, knows that I cannot thank him enough for his help at every phase of this research. It is no exaggeration to say that without his support, it would never have been done at all.

I am grateful to the Social Science Research Council who, through their Foreign Area Program, provided generous financial support for my research. They bear, of course, no responsibility either for its findings or for their interpretation which are entirely my own. I thank the editors of <u>Rural</u> <u>So-ciology</u> for permitting me to include some material that appeared earlier in that journal.

I am also indebted to the Department of Sociology of Louisiana State University and to the Louisiana State Agricultural Experiment Station who provided support for the preparation of the manuscript, and I am especially indebted to Lewis Watson, Pat Miller, Mercedes Davis, and Adrienne Craig who bore patiently with my demands during the typing of the manuscript and the typescript.

Finally, there are debts of a more personal sort. I am grateful to my parents who have always given generously both financial and moral support. This research is only the latest of many hurdles they have helped me to cross. I am especially grateful to my wife, Chintana. She willingly suspended her own career to allow this research to be carried out, and her patience and understanding during a difficult time have meant more to me than she can know.

Baton Rouge
May 1979

1. Historical Background

The civil service of Thailand is interesting
for many reasons. Thailand was the only Southeast
Asian society to retain its political independence
during the colonial period, and it is the only one
with an educated class of which most members speak
and read easily only their native language. Thai
economic and political development have taken place
within an unbroken cultural tradition, and therefore Thai official organizations provide an un-
usually favorable situation for the study of structural and cultural factors as they affect processes of social interaction. Moreover, the civil service is one of the most important sectors of Thai
society, and an understanding of its internal processes is of central importance to the understanding of the political changes that are taking place
in Thailand. This study describes some of these
changes as they manifest themselves at the local
level. In order to place the findings of the study
in a larger context, I begin with a brief introduction to the history and geography of Thailand.[1]

GEOGRAPHY

The country is a tropical one lying in the
center of the Southeast Asian peninsula. It is bor-
dered on the east by Laos and Cambodia, on the west
by Burma, and on the south by Malaysia. The heart
of Thailand is the valley of the Chao Phraya River,
a broad flat plain on which is grown the rice that
makes Thailand one of the largest exporters of that
commodity in the world. The plain is dotted with
villages strung out along the canals that provide
both water for agriculture and transport for the
products of the area. About one third of the

1

population of Thailand lives in the valley of the Chao Phraya, and more than half of the wealth of the country is produced there.

At the base of the plain, near the mouth of the river, lies the city of Bangkok, the economic and administrative capital of the country and its only real city. Bangkok is the principal deep water port and the only major center of industry in the country. Thailand has a long history of administrative centralization; the ancient kings tended to draw all economic and political activities into the capital and to discourage the development of other cultural centers in the kingdom. These tendencies were intensified in the modern period when the kings extended their control of the periphery of the kingdom in order to counter the colonial menace. The result has been an extraordinary concentration of urban population in Bangkok. In recent years the government has worked to reduce this concentration but without much seccess.

North of the central plain of Thailand is a mountainous region with narrow river valleys formed by the tributaries of the Chao Phraya. Rice is grown in the valleys, and orchards are beginning to be found on the hillsides. Lumbering is also an important activity there. The valleys are inhabited by Thais, but the mountians are inhabited by ethnically distenct tribal peoples who have never felt themselves to be a part of Thai society. Now, the government is attempting to integrate them into the society, but this has been difficult task and will continue to be a problem for some time.

The third major region, the northeast, is a relatively arid plateau drained by tributaries, not of the Chao Phraya, but the Mekong River. This is the poorest and most isolated part of the country. Although most of the people there grow rice, the region is poorly suited to its cultivation, and the government is trying to persuade the inhabitants to grow other crops. Some success has been achieved with kenaf (a crop similar to jute) and especially with maize which is now a major earner of foreign exchange for Thailand.

The south is a long penisula. It is a hilly region with fruit and rubber plantations. It is also the site of a substantial tin mining and smelting industry. The four southernmost provinces are inhabited by Malay speaking moslems. These people feel themselves to be foreigners in the Thai speak-

buddhist society of Thailand, and the area has some year been troubled by a separatist guerilla movement.

HISTORICAL BACKGROUND

Traditional Thai Government and Society

Thailand was a traditional southeast asian monarchy until the middle of the nineteenth century. She inherited a social and administrative system that had been formalized in the fifteenth century and had endured with few major changes for four hundred years. Under this system the king stood at the apex of society, and it existed to serve his needs. The Thai kings had in earlier days taken a fatherly interest in the welfare of their subjects, but the patriarchal conception of the kingship had been overlaid by the more autocratic and distant notion of the devaraja or devine king, a notion which was brought into Thailand by the court brahmins who were acquired from the Khmer Empire (Nivat, 1976).

Under this conception the king was held to occupy so exalted a status that he could not be approached by any but the highest of his subjects. Ordinary people had to shut their windows or face away when the king passed if they did not wish to risk being killed by one of his guards (Neher, 1966:5). Those who could approach him did so crawling and addressed him in an elaborate royal vocabulary derived from Sanskrit in which even the most ordinary actions of the king were given names that were different from their ordinary names. Thus, for instance, the usual polite word for the verb "to eat" in Thai was "t'an, but when the king or member of his family ate, the word was "sawoej". Most extreme was the phrase used instead of the pronoun for "you" when addressing the king. It translates roughly as "the dust under the royal foot which is upon my head." Even today, the royal vocabulary is used in newspaper accounts of the king's doings, and the ability to use it properly is one of the marks of an education person.

The extreme deference that was shown to the king generalized itself down the hierarchy of authority and prestige in society; at each level subordinates showed a deference to those above them that was proportional to the difference in their statuses. These patterns have changed very slowly.

3

As late as 1963 when I was a teacher in a secondary school in rural Thailand, female students would
walk up to within three feet of a teacher's desk
and then go down on their knees to approach closer,
and in 1973, when the research for this study was
carried out, elderly villagers would still squat
down in the dirt to address a high government official.

Under the king were two types of nobility.
First, there were the members of the royal family.
These were very numerous because of the institution
of the harem, but they were prevented from becom-
ing too numerous by a rule of declining descent.
The rule specified that descendents of a king had
a lower rank in each generation until at the fifth
generation they became commoners. The other type
of nobility consisted of the appointed officials
of the king. Official positions were in theory not
inheritable, but many of them, particularly the
governorships of remote provinces tended to become
inheritable in practice. Even in the capital, high
officials who were able to get their sisters or
sisters-in-law into the royal harem and their sons
and nephews accepted as royal pages were able to
secure their families' positions from generation
to generation (Wyatt, 1976).

The nobility were part of a system in which
every subject of the king was given rank which was
specified by a sakdi na number which referred in
principle to the number of rai (one rai = .4 acres
approximately) of land that an individual had the
right to cultivate. These numbers ran from twenty-
five rai for a free commoner to 100,000 rai for
royal prince in charge of a major department of
government. In between were the ranks of the various officials of the royal administration. The
sakdi na of the king was regarded as beyond calculation.

In this system, all of the subjects of the
king (except the members of the buddhist sangha,
or monastric order) were ranked within the same
hierarchy, which indicates that in an important
sense there was no real distinction between the
royal service and the larger society. Everyone
was in the royal service; for, the kingdom existed
to support and serve the king. Those who were
labeled as royal officials were simply the middle
ranks of the society, and, as such, they could
command the obedience of those below them, including the commoners who were subject to a corvee or
labor tax. They could be required to work for

4

the king or his officials for a specified number
of months each year. Each commoner was assigned
to a government department[2] for purposes of labor
mobilization. The officials of the department
were expected to use the labor to build such projects as canals or temples and to provide rice for
themselves and the king under the system known as
kin myang (to eat the place).

        This assigned right to use labor was the real
basis of power and wealth in ancient Thailand. We
who live in countries where land is a scarce resource are accustomed to thinking of its possession as conferring wealth and power, but Thailand
was, until very recently, a sparsely populated
country in which land was available freely to anyone who cared to clear and cultivate it. Even
quite close to the capital there were large areas
of jungle which were settled only in the late nineteenth century and then only by royally sponsored
colonization schemes. In such a situation the
possession of land was meaningless without the labor to cultivate it, and the power to command such
labor was monopolized by the kind and his officials. This fact, combined with the absence of
large cities based on trade (foreign trade was also
a monopoly of the king's) meant that there was no
class of people (except the buddhist monks who were
outside of politics) whose status was independent
of the king's will. There were no mercantile
class, no class of hereditary landowners, no independent professional associations, and no free
cities. The king could say with more justice than
Louis XIV ever could, "L'état, c'est moi."

        It followed that anyone who wanted to rise
in the world or to maintain a social status above
that of the lowers levels had to join the royal
service. There was no alternative. Consequently,
a career in the royal service came to be considered the career for a bright young man. Beginning in the latter part of the nineteenth century,
the kings of Thailand, who wanted to modernize
their country, enlarged the royal service and improved its technical capabilities. Thus, new
career opportunities were created in law, teaching,
medicine, administration, and a host of other
fields, but still these opportunities were in the
royal service. So, even today we find a pronounced
preference among educated Thais for careers in that
service.[3]

Moreover, even today, when the society of
Thailand has become much more differentiated than
it was in the nineteenth century, there is a sense
in which the royal service may still be seen as
synonomous with the middle ranks of Thai society.
For, the largest part of the development of private business and technical enterprise in Thailand
has been and continues to be in the hands of ethnic
Chinese immigrants and their children and grand-
children. Although most of these people are now
citizens of Thailand, there is a sense in which they
are regarded as 'not Thai'. From this perspective,
the Thai middle class is in the royal service.
    We have been considering the royal service of
Thailand in its structural aspect as a part of a
larger society. If we shift our focus to view that
service as a bureaucratic instrument of royal
policy, we will be struck by its very limited capacity to serve that function. Indeed, the old
royal service was rarely an instrument of royal
policy in the modern sense of the term for several
reasons. First, in a society like that of old
Thailand, the king did not really have many policies
in the sense of plans to direct the major economic
or social activities of the society. The people
existed to serve him, not the other way around, and
if he kept the kingdom reasonably free from bandits,
administered justice according to traditional religious conceptions, and avoided oppressive taxa-
tion, he was considered a good king. He was not
expected to develop policies.
    Moreover, the king was the prisoner of his own
exalted status. He could deal with conditions outside of his palace only through his ministers, and
they of course had their own interests and those of
their subordinates to consider. Finally, transportation and communication in the kingdom were extremely primitive. There were virtually no roads.
When the first missionaries went to the northern
town of Chiang Mai in the middle of the nineteenth
century, the trip took months, and in 1895 when
Prince Damrong, the first head of the reorganized
Ministry of the Interior, went on a tour of inspec-
tion of some of the provinces, he was informed that
no minister from the capital had ever made such a
tour before (Siffin, 1966:66). Indeed, most officials never left the capital, and they had no very
precise idea of where distant provinces were. No
maps of the kingdom existed, and the first survey
was conducted by a British team as a continuation of

6

the trigonometric survey of India in the eighteen-eighties. Under these circumstances, the king could not use the administrative system as an instrument of his will in a sustained way. He could galvanize it into action of a specific sort like resisting invasion or building a canal, and he could extract a certain amount of wealth, but beyond that he could not affect the lives of his people very much. They lived in their villages, cultivated their rice fields, and did the best they could to avoid the corvee when it became too onerous.

This system continued right down to the middle of the nineteenth century. At that time, Thailand was confronted with pressures from the expanding powers of Europe that could not be withstood by the traditional polity. Indeed, all of Thailand's neighbors succumbed and became colonies of one or another European power. The Thais were able to retain most of the attributes of sovereignty by a fortunate combination of circumstances. Of these the most important was that Thailand was blessed during this period with a series of strong, long-lived kings who were exceptionally well able to estimate the extent of the European menace and to deal with it.

King Mongkut ascended thr throne in 1851. He had expected to become king in 1824 when his father died, but he had been a monk at that time. So, his brother had become king in his stead, and Mongkut had remained a monk and had devoted himself to the study of Western learning. He had studied astronomy and navigation, geography, physics and chemistry, and the histories and contemporary characteristics of the major Western nations. So, when he became king, he could appreciate better than anyone in his kingdom the full extent of the European menace. He knew that the only way to deal with the Western nations was to accommodate them, to accede to their demands while at the same time modernizing and strengthening the kingdom. In treaties, he agreed to give up the royal monopoly of foreign trade, to limit import duties and to permit extraterritorial rights. He gave up territory to both the French and the British. Domestically, he modernized the coinage and substituted paid labor for corvee on royal projects. Most important of all, however, he had his children educated in English. They were the first generation of Thais to be education in a foreign knowledge.

The Reforms of King Chulalongkorn

King Mongkut was followed in 1873 by his son Chulalongkorn who completely reorganized the administration of the kingdom. He and his chief ministers constructed the system that we find today. King Chulalongkorn's father had succeeded through astute diplomacy in staving off the ruin which had overtaken his neighbors, but the son understood that major internal reforms would be necessary if he were to avoid losing his kingdom. He said,

> The greatest difficulty of the present day is the protection of our territory...Today we have Britain at our left and France at our right...We can no longer live in isolation as once we did. In our protection of the country three measures can be taken: Friendly diplomatic relations, the maintenance of defensive forces, and orderly administration. We will administer the country well if we foster opportunities for the people to earn livings so that they are benefited by the government. Then they will pay the taxes which are the economic foundation of the government. Consequently, an effective administration and a fostering of the ways of providing for the livelihood of the people are the most important, final purposes of the kingdom (Siffin, 1966:51).

To begin, with, the king made only modest reforms. In 1874, one year after ascending the throne, he appointed an official to be in charge of all revenues, and the following year he established a "Revenues Development Office" which ultimately grew into a full fledged ministry with responsibility for all revenue collection. The establishment of the Revenues Development Office followed upon an important speech which the king made to the State Council in which he explained the need for greater efficiency in the collection of revenue. He defended this policy by saying that the money was needed by the government for defense, salaries, public works, and internal improvements and not for his personal use.

This was a precedent shattering statement;

8

it was the first assertion in Thailand
that the primary responsibility of the
government was to the people, and it
implied that a distinction existed between crown and government funds, although this distinction was not made
official until later in the reign
(Vella, 1955:3).

The king also moved tentatively toward remuneration of officials by salaries and away from
kin muang. There had been a custom of giving annual gifts of money to the officials, and over the
years, the amounts of the gifts had tended to become standardized. The king continued the process
of standardization and, in addition, began the
practice of giving the gifts in monthly install-
ments.
Finally in April of 1892, King Chulalongkorn
issued the reorganization edict which changed the
basic structure of the government. Prior to the
reorganization, the government had been arranged
in six traditional ministries that combined functional and territorial responsibilities in a
variety of ways. Thus, for instance, the old Ministry of the Interior was in charge of the north
while the Ministry of Defense governed the south.
Justice was administered under various ministries,
and each ministry was responsible for raising its
own revenue under the kin muang system.
The king now established a set of modern,
functional ministries and brought the territorial
administration under a single ministry, that of the
Interior. He created a Ministry of Justice which
was eventually to take over the administration of
justice of the whole kingdom, and he established
a Ministry of Finance in which the responsibility
for collection of taxes and disbursement of revenue
was eventually to be concentrated.
However, it was not enough for the king to
set up a new formal organization of government. He
also had to see that it worked as he wanted it to.
In order to be able to do this, he had to be supported in his efforts at reform by his subordinates
at the highest levels. The old royal officials
had, for the most part, little understanding of
the menace of the West, and they were inclined to
be opposed to change (Wyatt, 1976:70). So, the
king turned to his relatives, among whom were
several men of truly exceptional ability, and they

became the heads of the new ministries. At the same time, the king moved gradually to provide modern training for the large numbers of middle level officers who would be required to man the new ministries as they expanded. Training schools for teachers, lawyers, physicians and administrators were established, and scholarships were given to exceptional students to study abroad.

King Chulalongkorn's successors in the early twentieth century continued the policy of training commoners to fill the middle levels of the royal service and at the same time reserving the highest levels for royal princes. In the long run, however, the policy was unworkable. The middle level officers were restive because they could not advance, and moreover many had learned democratic ideology as well as technical material while studying abroad. These dissatisfactions combined with the hardships brought on by the depression of the nineteen-thirties to produce the revolution of 1932 in which the absolute monarchy was overthrown. Today, the king is a figurehead, a symbol of national unity, and the real government of the country is a small group of military and civil officials.

The Contemporary Polity

Contemporary Thai politics reflect strongly the background described in the preceding section. One of the most important influences of the past is the lack of organized, popular, political parties with mass followings. The reason is partly that Thailand was never a colony. During the colonial period, the leaders of the other countries of the region felt a need to develop mass followings to aid in the struggle against the colonial masters. Since Thailand was never a colony, her leaders never felt such a need. In fact, they perceived the masses as needing guidance in a drive toward modernity that emanated entirely from the center.

The lack of political parties in the Western sense has been complemented by a general agreement among the elite groups on several important political principles. It would be fair to say that most Thai leaders agree on such points as that "communish" is a bad thing, that the Thai people are not yet "ready" for democracy, that the country ought to be strong militarily within her capabilities, that the economy ought to be stimulated, that the power of the chinese business community ought to be restrained, and so on. One result of this broad agreement within the elite has been that Thai politics has tended to be a politics of palace revolts and coups d'etat. Thailand experiences frequent changes of government, but these changes are not accompanied by changes in the policies of the government. They are simply changes in personnel.

In these shifts the army plays a key role. There is no reply to tanks and guns in a country which has no tradition of subordinating the military to the civilian government and in which all the members of the elite are reluctant to involve the masses in politics. Consequently, no government can survive without the support of the army, and high ranking military officers are always numerous in the prime ministers's cabinet, even when he is not a field marshal or a general himself, as he usually is.

The constituencies of the men in power consist of personal followings which have been called "cliques" (Wilson, 1966). The members of these cliques are for the most part holders of key positions in the civil and military bureaucracies. In the civil bureaucracies, these would include at a minimum the permanent under-secretaries and the heads of departments in the central administration and the governors of the provinces. These high ranking officials are in turn the heads of cliques at lower levels of the bureaucracy. Thus, one real base of power of the government is in the civil and military services.

Another pillar which supports the ruling group is the chinese business community. Most commercial activity in Thailand is in the hands of ethnic Chinese, and the political system provides no formal channel for the articulation of their interests. However, informal channels have evolved. The system is that a large business firm which wishes to be free of unpredictable government harassment incorporates itself and places one or more influential members of the ruling group on its board of directors. These men are paid handsome honoria for their trouble and they serve as channels for the articulation of business interests at high levels of government. (See Riggs, 1966, for a detailed description of this system.) At lower levels, small businessmen make an effort to cultivate good personal relations with local officials as is described below in Chapter Five.

Thus, political action in Thailand is narrowly based and highly personal. Issues are raised, not as the demands of organized interest groups, but as requests for favors from individual clients to individual patrons. This has certain advantages for those who have access to influential patrons, but it completely excludes those who do not. Moreover, the system tends to create organizational ties that are vertical rather than horizontal. Just as under the old regime organizations that compete with the central government for power are discouraged, and a hierarchical dependence on it is encouraged.

Finally, we should note one more holdover from traditional Thai society in the contemporary polity Action in old Thailand was always supposed to be initiated from the top. There was no provision in the ancient polity for the legitimate exercise of power from the bottom up as there is in the democratic polities of the West. A subordinate could ask a superior for a favor, but he could not bring pressure for a policy. Even today, the notion that action ought to originate at the top is strongly felt by many Thai people. This is gradually changing because new sources of power are emerging in the society as a result of economic development and its accompanying social change, but in rural areas, like the one where this research was done, the change comes slowly. Today, the officials of the provincial and district administration still feel a paternal responsibility for the people entrusted to their care, and the latter are expected to defer in policy matters to the judgment of their superiors.

The Events of 1973 and Their Aftermath

The political system that I have described has been a good deal shaken during the last few years. In the fall of 1973 a government was forced out of power by a mass movement, in this case a movement of students. The events were roughly as follows: Thailand was ruled at that time by a group whose leading members were Marshal Thanom, General Prapart (usually regarded as the real strong man), and Colonel Narong, who was Thanom's son and Prapart's son-in-law. That fall, several university students and teachers were arrested for remarks critical of the regime, and a movement was organized by students in Bangkok to demonstrate

12

peacefully to demand the release of those who had been arrested. Large numbers of students came in from institutions all over Thailand, and a very large but peaceful demonstration took place on Saturday, October 14. Someone in the government, allegedly Colonel Narong, panicked, and the students were fired on. A large number were wounded, and a few were killed. The students then erected barricades in a part of the city and burned some buildings, including the home of the national lottery, that were symbolic of the evils of the regime. There was fighting between the police and the students. The army and police surrounded the barricaded area and sealed it off.[4]

That was the situation on Saturday night. On Sunday morning the government abdicated, and Thanom, Prapart, and Narong left the country. A caretaken government was formed under a respected lawyer and was given the responsibility of drafting a constitution. This was done, and elections for the new legislature were duly held in January of 1975. However, these elections showed that in some ways not very much had changed. Many political parties competed in the election, but each of them was composed of the personal cliques of its leaders. No party had a mass following, and the result was that of none had a majority in the new parliament. So, a coalition government was formed under Seni Pramoj, an elderly and conservative cousin of the king. However, his government was unable to govern the country, and when it fell Seni was succeeded by his brother Kukrit, also and elderly and conservative man. He included in his cabinet a number of high ranking military officers, some of whom had been important political figures for decades. Kukrit was succeeded by general. In short, it appeared on the surface at least that little had changed but the personnel.

However, during 1974 a number of things happened that indicated that perhaps some change would be needed. First, a number of labor unions, previously illegal, were formed in Bangkok in certain industries, and there were strikes. Second, during the year several delegations of farmers appeared at the Ministry of the Interior to request assistance against money lenders in rural areas. Finally, guerrilla activities in various parts of the country became more open and widespread. At the same time, the excellent economic conditions that Thailand had experienced for a

decade and a half came to an end. The rise in the
price of oil and the withdrawal of American troops
occurred at the same time, and the effects were
widespread inflation and unemployment. Thus, the
ruling circles experienced a sharp increase in the
pressure to "go public," to build popular support
by creating mass political parties. Whether this
will be done on a scale sufficiently broad to prevent a change in the regime more serious than any
that has yet occurred remains to be seen. The record of regimes in other countries in similar situations is a dismal one, but the Thais have shown
over the years a remarkable flexibility, and they
may succeed where others have failed.

THE STRUCTURE OF CONTEMPORARY THAI SOCIETY

Villages and Urban Centers

     Thai society is overwhelmingly rural with
nearly 80 percent of its labor force engaged in
agriculture. Of the various crops grown in Thailand, rice is by far the most important in terms of
area planted and of number of people employed in
its production. Rice is the staple food of the
Thai people, both rural and urban, and a majority
of the population of the country are directly engaged in growing it. The "typical" Thai is a
peasant rice farmer who lives in a village.
     There are two major types of Thai villages.
Some villages, especially in the central plain, are
line villages that are built along canals or other
waterways with the rice fields stretching out be-
hind the houses. The other type of village is
common in dryer areas and consists of a cluster of
houses with the rice fields around them. Settle-
ments in which farmers live scattered, each on his
own farm, are common only in a few areas in the
lower central plain and in the rubber growing areas
of the south and southeast.
     In earlier years, most Thai villages were
isolated and fairly self sufficient communities.
Commercialization of agriculture and monetization
of the rural economy were quite limited. However,
over the last couple of decades the government has
carried on a vigorous program of road construction,
and now most villages are connected to their district capitals by roads that are passable by four
wheel drive vehicles most of the time and by ordinary vehicles during the dry season. Consequently,

14

today most Thai farmers are engaged to some degree
in commercial farming, although they still consume
a part of their crop directly, and many products
that used to be made at home are now bought in the
market.

In village society most people live in nu-
clear family households. Thailand does not have a
tradition of large, extended family households in
peasant villages except that when a woman marries
she and her husband often reside with her parents
while accumulating the wealth needed to set up on
their own. One of the daughters, in principle the
youngest, remains with the parents, and she and her
husband inherit the family house and compound. The
bilateral kindred is also an important group in
Thai society. Relatives often help one another
with tasks like the rice harvest, extend loans of
money to one another, and assist each other in times
of crisis. However, the bilateral kindred is not
a corporate group. Rather, it is a collection of
people from which a smaller group of those of with
whom one exchanges assistance may be chosen.

There are very few formal organizations or
associations in Thai villages, a fact which has led
some students to describe Thai society as having a
"loose" social structure (Dieter-Evers, 1969). However, Potter (1976) has shown that this is a distortion of the data. Thai peasant social life is
tightly organized in a number of ways. One way is
through the relationship between juniors and
seniors. Great respect is paid by young people to
their seniors, and benefits are frequently obtained
by a sort of patronage system in which juniors gave
deference and obedience in exchange for help and
protection. When a wealthy villager is especially
good at attracting juniors to him by this means, he
may become the head of an "entourage" (Potter, 1976:
193) which may in turn provide the basis for a
political faction within the village.

Sex is also a major organizing principle in
Thai village society. Women and men do not spend
much time in each other's company, and work is done
either by members of one sex or of the other. The
major exceptions to this are the periods of very
heavy labor demand in the cultivation of rice. Women
and men work together during the planting, trans-
planting, harvesting, and threshing. However,
while women and men are generally segregated in
their activities, women are no secluded. There is
no purdah in Thai society.

Women are subordinate to men in principle, and wives are generally deferent to their husbands, at least in public. On the other hand, the subordination of women is limited by the fact that they control a great deal of their families' cash income. Many village women sell their families' vegetables and fruit in the commune or district market. This is almost exclusively a women's activity. Men rarely engage in selling agricultural produce except for the sale of the rice crop itself, and one must remember that most Thai farmers eat a large part of the rice they produce. Moreover, even the money that is earned from the sale of rice is often given to the wife to keep. So, women have more power in their families than their overt deference would seem to indicate.

There are also extrafamilial social ties based on reciprocal labor exchanges. Individuals harvesting and threshing the rice or for big projects like building houses. However, labor exchanges of this type are gradually being replaced by hired labor as both commercialization and inequality increase in the villages. Labor mobilization on a village-wide basis occurs more rarely. It is used to repair or maintain the village temples, roads, bridges, or schools. In the north, villages in some places have elaborate village irrigation systems that are built and maintained by voluntary village labor, but in the central region such irrigation systems do not exist because the flatness of the land renders small scale irrigation systems difficult to construct while large ones would be beyond the organizational capacity of a single village.

Above the village administratively is the commune (<u>tambon</u>), but the commune is not a different social level; it is simply a group of villages. In contrast, the step above the commune, which is the district, marks a substantial social transition. The district is the lowest level of the regular national administration, and the officials who live in a district center set the social tone of the place. To serve the officials, the district also has a number of shops and restaurants which are generally owned and operated by Chinese immigrants or their children. It also has a branch of the post office and one of the government savings bank. It it is a large district, it may even have one or more private banks.

16

Above the district is the province. The provincial capital is similar to the district center
in the sorts of people who live in it, but its
population is likely to be much larger and the number and variety of services offered correspondingly
greater. It also has the provincial courts and a
modern hospital. However, no provincial capital
is a really large town. In 1971, only six had
populations over 50,000, and none had a population
over 100,000 (Romm, n.d.:5).

There is an enormous difference in income and
level of living between the townsfolk and the village people on the average. For, while nearly 80
percent of the employed population is in agriculture, they produce only 31 percent of the gross
domestic product (Ingram, 1971:235). However, one
should not assume that most people in the towns are
rich. The low level of living in agriculture and
the rapid rate of growth of the population keep the
wage level low--less than a dollar a day outside
of Bangkok. So, although most rich people live in
the towns, not everyone there is rich. Moreover,
the wealth is not evenly distributed among towns.
In general, provincial capitals are much wealthier
than mere district capitals, and Bangkok is
enormously wealthier than any provincial capital.

Bangkok is, in fact, the only real city in
Thailand. Some three and a half million people
live there. The city contains 77 percent of the
nation's telephones, consumes eighty-two percent
of its electricity, and a generates 82 percent of
its business taxes and 73 percent of its personal
income taxes (Romm, n.d.:7). Bangkok is the focus
of the rail and road systems, contains a large
proportion of the institutions of higher education
and is the center of political power.

Many officials want to live in Bangkok, although it is less comfortable and much more expensive to live there than in a provincial town.
This is partly due to the excitement of living in
an urban center that is the center of the intellectual life of the kingdom and partly due to the
alleged superiority of the schools in Bangkok. The
latter reason is important because education is the
principal road to advancement in Thai society, and
most officials want their children to have the best
possible chances of success. The graduates of the
best schools in Bangkok regularly do better on the
university entrance examinations than do the graduates of other schools, and parents hope to be able

17

to send their children to one of these good schools
without having to bear the expense of supporting
them away from home. However, the most important
reason for wanting to live in Bangkok is that it
is the center of the administrative system. An
ambitious official can become personally acquainted
with his superiors who control his future only if
he is stationed in Bangkok, and therefore he re-
gards at least some periods of duty there as essential to his career.

Education, Status, and Power in Thai Society

From the viewpoint of the civil servants
whose activities are the subject of this study,
Thai society may be seen as being divided into two
major groups; the educated and uneducated. This
distinction connotes much more in Thailand than it
does in the United States. To be educated means
not only to have mastered technical material as it
does to us but also to have mastered the social and
linguistic forms that educated people use. Being
educated in Thai society also connotes a certain
social position. Traditionally, there were only
two types of education, that which prepared one for
the royal service and that which was received by
the monks whose status was even higher than that
of the royal officials. Even today, most educated
Thais outside the sangha or buddhist order aspire
to be civil or military officials.

Among the uneducated, there are four major
groups outside of the national capital. They are
the urban poor (including casual laborers, trishaw
drivers, and the like), most craftsmen, most
chinese businessman, and the peasants who are by
far the most numerous. The educated include virtually all officials, a few independent professionals, the managerial and clerical employees of
such modern private businesses as banks, and a few
large plantation owners. These last are found
generally in the southern and southeastern parts
of the country where rubber and fruit are grown on
plantations, and even there they are exceptional.
In Bangkok, there is an additional group in the
educated class. This group is what has been called
the "old elite" (Wilson, 1966:53). It consists of
titled aristocrats of the old regime and members
of the royal family. Since no titles have been
given since 1932, and the harem was abolished
earlier in this century, the old elite is gradually
disappearing.

NOTES

1. This chapter contains a very brief, general introduction to Thai society and politics. For the reader who wants more detailed information, there are several good sources. A good general book is Frank J. Moore's Thailand: its people, its society, its culture, New Haven, Human Relations Area Files Press, 1974. For information on peasant life and social organization, see John E. de Young's Village Life in Modern Thailand, Berkeley, University of California Press, 1955, or the more recent book by Jack M. Potter. Thai Peasant Social Structure, Chicago, University of Chicago Press, 1976. Two good general works on Thai politics are David A. Wilson's Politics in Thailand, Ithaca, Cornell University Press, 1962, and Fred W. Riggs' Thailand; the modernization of a bureaucratic polity, Honolulu, East-West Center Press, 1966. A good general study of the Thai civil service is William J. Siffin's The Thai Bureaucracy: institutional change and development, Honlulu, East-West Center Press, 1966. The best general work on the Thai economy is James C. Ingram's Economic Change in Thailand: 1850-1970, Stanford, California, Stanford University Press, 1971.

2. This is a simplified presentation which takes no account of the distinction between p'rai luang and p'rai song.

3. The words "royal service" instead of "civil service" are used advisedly; the Thai term for a civil servant is "k'arachakan" which means a servant of the king.

4. More or less. I was staying in a hotel in the area at the time, and I managed to drive there through some side streets.

2. Theoretical Perspective

The social changes that were discussed in the last chapter have had profound effects on the Thai civil service. The economic development of the Thai countryside has brought new social classes to political importance, and at the same time, the government's desire to strengthen its hold on the rural areas has made it increasingly responsive to some of their demands. So, the local representatives of Thailand's 'bureaucratic polity' have had to adapt to new conditions. In addition, development has brought Western trained professionals to rural Thailand. These professionals have goals and standards that are incompatible with the traditional organization of the civil service that employs them. Their ideals of professional autonomy and collegial administration have altered profoundly the functioning of the organizations they serve. This study examines the behavior of two types of officials: administrators and professionals. Administrators are represented by the staff of a district office and professionals by the physicians in a provincial hospital.

Thai officials, like others, try to maximize the rewards and satisfactions of their roles, but their efforts are limited and constrained by the structural and cultural features of their work situations. Structural features consist of concrete, historically developed relationships among persons and among groups which the individual finds in his work situation and which he must take as givens in constructing his own line of action. I will examine the effects of two structural features of the Thai civil service on the behavior of its officials. These features include: (1) the distribution of various sorts of power among officials, and (2) the nature of the incentive system of the civil service.

Cultural features are the norms and expectations which govern the actions of people in their
work situation. Such norms include both the norms of
specific professional or organizational groups and
those of the larger society of which the groups are
parts. I will examine the effects on Thai official
behavior of four cultural features of the Thai civil
service and society. These features include (1) professionalism - the nature of Thai medical professionalism and its effect on physicians' behavior;
(2) norms of deference governing interpersonal relations between subordinates and superiors and among
equals; (3) norms governing the expression of regard
and the symbolic means for maintaining trust; (4)
norms governing prior relationships in Thai society,
especially graduation from a common university.

Because structural and cultural factors con-
strain individual behavior, regular patterns emerge.
Officials in certain positions regularly employ certain means to reach their ends because those are the
means available to them. By the same token, officials in positions which differ significantly in
terms of the structural or cultural factors mentioned above display significantly different patterns of behavior. This study will focus on these
stable patterns and will explore possible explanations for the differences and similarities among
them. I will ignore idiosyncratic variations in
style because discussion of them would obscure rather than illuminate the basic relationships under
investigation.

Relatively little research has been directed
toward the study of social exchange or other interaction processes in Thai organizations. Works by
political scientists have discussed the world view,
attitude toward authority, and self concept of the
Thai bureaucrat, and in general these studies have
stressed the importance of hierarchical and defer-
ential values and the relative unimportance of norms
of productivity in explaining the behavior of Thai
officials (Riggs, 1966; Siffin, 1966; Wilson, 1962).
Previous authors have also discussed the importance
of patron-client bonds and of vertically integrated
cliques in the informal structure of Thai administrative and political organizations. Stress has been
laid on the relative lack of organization among
equals as compared with that between patrons and
clients.

Important field studies of Thai administration
include Horrigan's (1959) study of local government
and administration, Meksawan's (1961) study of the

role of the provincial governor and Neher's (1969) study of decision making and resource allocation at the district level. Samudavanija's (1971) study of budgetary processes and Wichaidit's (1973) study of provincial administration rely on a combination of library sources with the authors' extensive personal experience in Thailand. All of the above researchers have been interested in government and administration rather than in interaction or social exchange as topics of research in their own right. Nevertheless, their works contain a number of findings on the relationships among superiors and subordinates at the district and provincial levels. In general, they agree that the governor lacks staff assistance and that therefore he is led to construct personal lines of communications. The studies also find that there are difficulties in the relationships between the administrative generalists and the technical specialists that result from the ambiguity of the distribution of authority. The importance of participation in ceremonials and other activities designed to gain the confidence and cooperation of the citizens is also supported by these researchers. Finally, they agree that advancement for a provincial official depends on a combination of hard work directed toward dramatic, highly visible projects and the cultivation of good personal relations with superiors.

The work of Rubin (1974) is more closely relevant to the concerns of this study. He analyzes various modes of communication among officials, especially that between superiors and subordinates, in maintaining group solidarity and in assuring the efficient accomplishment of tasks. This study supports Rubin's findings, and, in addition, places them in the context of the efforts of officials to build satisfying roles. More specific points of agreement and disagreement between my findings and those of other students of Thai official behavior will be discussed as they arise in later chapters.

SOCIAL EXCHANGE IN ORGANIZATIONS

This study analyzes the behavior of Thai officials from the perspective of "social exchange" theory as developed by Blau (1964), Homans (1961), and others. The notion that social interaction can be viewed in terms of exchange has proved a very fruitful one in the study of organizational behavior in the United States (See Blau, 1963; Lawrence and Lorsch, 1967; Perrow, 1964; March and Simon, 1958 among many others). Researchers in other societies have also used this perspective (Marsh and Mannari, 1971; Cole, 1971; Crozier, 1964; Taub, 1969).

Several students of Thai society have discussed exchange processes. Riggs (1966) and Siffin (1966) give great importance to social exchange in vertical cliques in the informal structures of Thai official organizations, and Shor (1962) speaks of the "entre-preneurial strategy" of Thai officials in building their careers. In general these researchers show the importance in social exchange of two major structural factors: the distribution of power based on the control of scarce resources and the incentive system of the organization which determines the actors' goals.

With some notable exceptions (Goffman, 1961; Strauss, 1962; Cole, 1971), social exchange theorists have emphasized the role of exchange in the building of social structure. Following in the tradition of Blau and Homans, exchange has been viewed as a basic social process out of which social structures emerge. Relations among individuals have been of concern, not for themselves, but for their social structural consequences. This study takes the opposite perspective: social exchange in organizations is seen as taking place within an already structured social environment which places narrow constraints on the behavior of actors, and the question to be answered is what are the consequences of these constraints for the roles that actors can build for themselves? Or, to put it somewhat differently, how do the structural and cultural features of actors' organizational situations limit and channel the social exchange processes among officials into regular, predictable patterns?

Before answering this question it may be well to define the term "social exchange" more closely. Some theorists have used the term to mean something essentially like economic exchange. The actor is represented as toting up in his head the costs and benefits of a certain contribution to a relationship and then making that contribution only if the benefits exceed the costs. This view of social exchange requires, if not full knowledge of the consequences that an act might have, at least that an unambiguous benefit and cost be assigned by an actor to each of his actions.

In certain relationships, however, there are norms which prevent the actor from assigning prices to his contributions. An example of such a relationship is friendship. If I see a friend walking when I am driving, I am supposed to offer him a ride, not with the expectation of a specific return but as an expression of our friendship and I am not expected to assign any specific value to the favor I have done for him. Nevertheless, if over a long period I do him many such favors, and he fails to find occasions to reciprocate, I am likely to begin to doubt the genuineness of his regard for me, to feel exploited, and to be less ready to help him in the future. This is not to say that friendship is somehow a lie cloaking a crass economic reality. The point is that friends are supposed to be able to count on each other for assistance when it is needed, and those who fail to show that their credit is good in this respect are regarded as "fair weather friends."

I will use the term "social exchange" to refer to the sort of exchange that characterizes friendships following Goffman's (1961:275) usage. Social exchange differs from economic exchange in that in the former no prices are set on particular items exchanged. Instead, there is only a rough appreciation of the value of each contribution. Moreover, in social exchange actors are oriented toward the purchase of specific items of present or future assistance. Nevertheless, rough calculations of the value of each person's contributions to a relationship permit him and his friends to know when he is not "pulling his weight."

Social exchange characterizes many relationships besides friendship. Indeed, straightforward economic exchange is the exception rather than the rule in human affairs. The reason is that usually we are not in a position to pay for assistance we need, either because the price would be beyond our means or because we have nothing to offer that a potential helper wants at the moment when we want his assistance. In social exchange, we tacitly offer unspecified services to be given on demand or even at need without demand.[1] This is to say that we offer to enter into a stable relationship of some sort with the other. Such relationships may include those of colleagues, of spouses, of club members, or patrons and clients, as well as those of friends. Different sorts of relationships imply different sorts of things being exchanged, of course. In fact, from one point of view, different sorts of relationships may be defined by the sorts of things that are exchanged in them.

TRUST IN SOCIAL EXCHANGE

The value to another of our offer of unspecified services on demand depends on his estimate of
our trustworthiness. If he believes that we really
can be counted on, he will be inclined to accept our
offer and to meet our request for his help. At the
beginning of a relationship a difficulty arises
which is that it is hard to form an estimate of the
trustworthiness of a stranger. It is risky to do a
favor for a stranger because there is no way of
knowing whether he will reciprocate, but if the favor is small, then the risk is small. Consequently,
relationships between strangers are usually built up
slowly through small exchanges in which each has opportunities to test the trustworthiness of the other
without incurring much risk.

The difficulty of establishing trust is increased by the fact that the time when one receives
a favor may not be followed soon by an occasion to
repay it. So, each party to an ongoing social exchange relationship must do something to maintain
the other's belief that he will pay when a suitable
occasion arises. Therefore, each expresses by a wide
variety of symbolic gestures the fact that he is
conscious of his social debts and that he cares
about the relationship. Each asks about the other's
health when they meet and desires particularly to
know about the welfare of the other's family. One
asks the other out for a beer, and the other pro-
poses that they go on a picnic together. Such expressions of concern and liking are, of course, rewarding to the one who receives them, but they also
serve a symbolic function. They convey the message,
"I have no immediate occasion to do you a favor, but
should you need one you know that I am your friend."

The risk attached to the early stages of building a relationship with a stranger may also be reduced by choosing someone whom we have some prior
reason to trust. Generally, there are two categories
of such reasons. First, one may trust another because of a prior relationship or common identity
that one shares with him. Persons who have a prior
relationship or who share a common identity can
build trust more easily because the trustworthiness
they attribute to each other initially will make it
easier for each of them to find out if the other is
really trustworthy (Dalton, 1959; Kruglanski, 1970).
Such relationships or identities as common family
membership, ethnic background, or graduation from
a common school can serve as bases for an initial

level of trust; some fraternal orders like the Massons serve this function (Dalton, 1959:150-5), and in India common caste membership is used (Taub, 1969:189).

Another way of reducing the risk of trusting strangers in some relationships is by relying on people who are known to abide by norms of professional conduct. It is widely believed in some societies that professionals are to be trusted to live up to professional norms when they are acting in their professional capacities. This means that one may trust a professional in certain professional capacities even if one is not personally acquainted with him. Thus, for example, a patient may trust his physician or a client his lawyer, and of course professionals may trust each other.

There are, then, three alternative strategies for creating trust among associates. They are (1) the reliance on prior relationships or shared identities, (2) the reliance on commitments to norms of professional conduct, and (3) the gradual building of trust through social exchange. These strategies may be used singly or in combination. Most commonly, some combination of either (1) or (2) and (3) is preferred. That is, one tries to avoid placing trust in people who cannot be trusted either for reason (1) or for reason (2), but one does not trust equally everyone who fits those categories. Higher levels of trust are reserved for those who have given direct evidence of trustworthiness.

At this point it is important to note that the choice of a trust-building strategy has implications for the sorts of relationships one can build. This is because in a given culture there are norms regarding the sorts of exchanges which it is proper to make in a given relationship. There are things which it is reasonable to ask one's wife to do, for example, and things which she can be expected to refuse, and the same holds for one's friends, old school pals, clients, business associates, or professional colleagues. The basis on which trust is established places limits on the content and dependability of social exchange in relationships and consequently on the sorts of relationships actors can build within a given context.

For example, basing trust on the belief that certain types of persons will adhere to norms of professional conduct may be consequential in several ways in Thailand as elsewhere. First, as we shall see, professional role definitions are relatively narrow. Professionals do not recognize the sorts of

26

of diffuse obligations to superiors that most civil
servants in Thai society accept. Thus, for example,
the director of a hospital in Thailand cannot expect
to receive from his staff the kinds of personal
services that district officials give to their
superior, the district officer, as a matter of
course

Second, professionals demand and are accorded
a degree of autonomy in their work which few nonprofessional civil servants can expect. A superior
cannot exert as much control over professionals as
he does over line administrators, or if he does, he
must be prepared for a good deal of conflict. Among
physicians in the United States, the conflict between bureaucratic norms and the professional norm
of autonomy has led to the establishment of the well
known dual hierarchy of control (Goss,1963) in
which physicians submit to bureaucratic supervision
only in areas defined as nonmedical.

Moreover, a professional tends to be committed
to his work, his clients, and his professional colleagues rather than to his organization or to his
superiors. Therefore, his doing good work cannot
serve as a basis for his supervisor's attributing
loyalty to him (Gouldner, 1957; Wilensky, 1956).
Furthermore, it is difficult to fit the professional
into an organizational clique because he often cannot be rewarded by promotion to an administrative
post. Bureaucratic career ladders provide for increasing status within an organization while professionals are primarily concerned with status within their respective occupations   (Goldner and Ritti,
1967; Gouldner, 1957; Hall, 1968; Miller, 1967).
Promotion of professionals to executive positions is
often resisted by them because they do not want to
lose the opportunity to practice their professions.
Therefore, it is very difficult for professionals to
build administrative roles in organizations. They
will be trusted by their colleagues in professional
matters but generally not in others.

Professionalism is a Western concept, and no
comparable notion existed in traditional Thai society. The absolutism of the old Thai monarchy left no
room for corporate professional groups or for
sources of authority that were in principle independent of the royal will. However, modern Thailand has
acquired several Western professions in the course
of modernization. Thai schools of law, medicine,
education, engineering, and social work have been
organized along American or European lines and par-
tially staffed with American and European faculty.

Professional associations like the Thai Medical Association and Kurusapha (a teachers' association) have been formed. But the development of professionalism in Thailand has taken place in a very different historical context from that in which professionalism developed in the West, as will be described in more detail in Chapter Six. As yet, no study has been made of the meaning of professionalism in Thai society except Bryant's (1969) brief, impressionistic survey of Thai medicine. Nothing is known of how professionalism affects the day-to-day behavior of Thai professionals.

This study will investigate the influence of professionalism on the behavior of physicians, a highly professionalized group in Thailand. Most Thai physicians practice as full time civil servants on the staffs of government hospitals. Each province has at least one such hospital, and these hospitals fall under the same general regulations and have the same formal relationships with the provincial and central administration as other official government agencies in provincial Thailand. This study will investigate the differences between a Thai civil service organization employing professionals (e. g., a provincial hospital) and one employing nonprofessionals (e. g., a district administrative office). Because of the administrative similarities between the civil service structure of the hospital and the civil service structure of the district office, the organizational context within which the professional and nonprofessional or bureaucratic officials construct their roles will be held reasonably constant. A more detailed discussion of the organizations chosen as research sites and of the reasons for choosing them is contained in the Appendix. The substantive problems of professionalism and its consequences are discussed in Chapters Six and Seven where the data are analyzed.

OTHER FACTORS AFFECTING SOCIAL EXCHANGE IN ORGANIZATIONS

Social exchange is affected not only by the basis on which trust is established but also by a number of other structural and cultural variables which act to limit and channel the process in specific directions. This study will examine the effects of several such variables, and therefore we now turn our attention to a discussion of them.

Structural Factors

Each official engages freely in social exchange and endeavors to build a line of action that suits him, but he does not do so in a situation of his own making. The other actors in the situation are not randomly placed around him. Instead, he finds them already organized into a social structure that consists of relationships which they have built up and in which they have some stake. A good deal has been invested by the actors in constructing their relationships with one another, and therefore attempts to alter the social structure will be resisted.

There are two major types of structural limitations on role making in organizations which are (1) the distribution of power and (2) the structure of incentives. The ability of an official to build his role to suit himself depends on his power relative to that of others around him. In this study Emerson's (1962) definition of power is used in preference to Blau's (1964) definition. That is, the power of A over B equals the dependence of B on A for some reward. In a relationship of unequal power, it is not regarded as a net quantity. That is, the power of A over B is not net of the power of B over A. Consequently, even in an unequal relationship, we may speak of the power of each of the actors over the other.

The relative power of workers in organizations to define their roles as they would like can vary enormously. Some, like assembly line workers (Chinoy, 1955), have virtually no power except through union negotiations; some, like printers (Blauner, 1964) have considerable power; a few, like physicians, (Goss, 1963; Strauss et al., 1963) have nearly complete control.

In general, there are three sources of power for officials: (1) control of a scarce resource, (2) control of the flow of information, and (3) the ability to deal with uncertainty in the environment. (For general discussions of these, see Mechanic, 1962; Cyert and March, 1963; Perrow, 1961; Lawrence and Lorsch, 1967; Thompson, 1967; and Hickson et al., 1971 among many others.) The control of scarce resources is an important base of power in Thai organizations. It is quite common for an official at the district level, for instance, to require the help of another in paying a social debt to a citizen. Thus, an official who is in a position to be of service to citizens is powerful in his relations with other officials at the district office where inducements must be provided for citizens to participate in the district's development programs.

Control of the flow of information is also important. The organizational obstacles to the upward flow of information have been amply documented (Hall, 1972; Dalton, 1959). In some organizations, good information simply cannot be obtained by superiors at all (Crozier, 1964). This occurs because bureaucratic regulations have removed from superiors the discretion necessary for them to reward subordinates differentially, and therefore no one has any incentive to make special contributions. In Thai organizations, it has been by more than one researcher that superiors have great difficulty in getting good information about the progress of work in the field (Horrigan, 1959; Meksawan, 1961). Reporting arrangements are inadequate, and high level officials try to deal with this problem by building cliques of subordinates whom they can trust and from whom they get information. This clearly indicates that information is an important source of power in the Thai civil service.

The ability to deal wit uncertainty is also a source of power. Crozier (1964:158) argues that in an organization each member tries to bind the others with rules to remove their discretion while maintaining his own freedom from restriction. He does so because power depends on the possession of discretion. A person without discretion cannot make his behavior contingent on the responses of another and so cannot influence the other. Those who deal with uncertain factors in the environment must be allowed discretion precisely because they deal with unpredictable contingencies. Having discretion, they can use it to reward or punish others, and consequently such persons are always powerful (Wilensky, 1956; Lawrence and Lorsch, 1967).

In Thai civil service agencies, the main source of uncertainty comes from difficulties in obtaining resources to carry out the agency's programs and to reward subordinates. An official who, through his relations with highly placed persons in the central administration of his ministry in Bangkok or through his relations with citizens, is able to procure resources is powerful in his relations with other officials.

Cutting across the above issues is the question of ambiguity or unclarity in the location of power in the line. If power does not descend in a single, clear chain of command, there will be opportunities

30

for conflict among the various power holders. This is a problem in the Thai civil service, as has been observed by several researchers (Meksawan, 1961; Horrigan, 1959; Siffin, 1966). The division of responsibility between the administrative generalists who govern territorial units and the heads of technical sections is quite ambiguous. This may be either a source of difficulty for a Thai official or an opportunity for him to exploit in building his role; often it is both.

In addition to the question of the ambiguity of the chain of command, there is also the issue of centralization of decision making. In Thai official organizations, decision making power is often located at a considerable social and physical distance from the officials who carry out the decisions. Field officials ordinarily cannot decide but only propose. Given the difficulties that high level officials have in obtaining needed information, this centralization clearly places a premium on trust between superiors and subordinates. The latter must make every effort to build their superiors' trust in order not to be subjected to long delays in decisions to approve requests or recommendations. This study will investigate the effects of the above aspects of the distribution of power on the role making of Thai officials.

The other type of structural element that constrains social exchange in an organization is its system of incentives. One element of this system is the size of the rewards that officials at all levels receive. If the rewards are too small, officials may only do the amount of work that they judge to be a fair return for their salaries.[2] In such a case, superiors may have to find informal ways of rewarding their subordinates, or it may be necessary to permit a certain amount of bribery or corruption. It is also important to know the probability of receiving a reward for good work. It may be, for example, that good work leads to promotions, but this is not always the case. If it is not, some workers may prefer leisure to hard work. We also want to know what sort of work is rewarded, and how the reward system relates to the values of the workers. For example, one of Blau's (1963) findings concerned the effect of statistical record keeping on the job performance of employment service interviewers. He found that workers spent their efforts on doing the things that would look good on their monthly reports, which meant maximizing the number of job placements they made. This conflicted, however, with professional

norms of trying to help workers find jobs that suited them· and of providing needed counseling service
to workers. Such a consequence could not help but
undermine the interviewers' commitment to professional norms in the long run and so change the terms
of social exchange among them.

All of these aspects of the incentive system
are important in explaining the character of social
exchange among Thai officials. Their salaries are
too low (Horrigan, 1959), good work is not consistently rewarded (Horrigan, 1959), and certain kinds
of work, notably dramatic, highly visible projects,
are more likely to be rewarded than other sorts of
work, especially when the highly visible projects
are combined with the exercise of certain political
and interpersonal skills (Neher, 1969). This study
will investigate the effects of this situation. In
addition to the limitations on individual freedom
which originate in the social structure, there are
also limitations based on cultural prescriptions and
proscriptions, and to these we now turn.

Cultural Limitations on Social Exchange

Cultural limitations on social exchange consist
of norms and expectations that are held by members
of the culture within which an individual lives and
works. Such norms include, for example, the pre-
scribed deference due to superiors. If, as is the
case in Thailand, custom prescribes that subordinates must always give great deference to their superiors, then the expression of deference can neither be used by subordinates to reward superiors (as
Blau, 1963:141, argues) nor by superiors as a sign
of trustworthiness.

Similarly, the forms of ingratiation vary from
one cultural setting to another. Jones (1964) reviews research on the ways in which a person can in-
gratiate himself with another, and the conditions
under which he will fail to do so. The evidence he
presents supports the view that ingratiation will
fail if the rewards proffered by the ingratiator
are too great because he will be suspected of being
what he is. Thus, for example, it is customary in
Thailand for some subordinates to visit their superiors at home occasionally. An official who does this
gives his superior a chance to send him on errands
or employ him in other ways and thus to give the
subordinate a chance to display his commitment to
his work and his loyalty to his superior. If, howev-

32

er, the subordinate visits too often, the Thais call it "going in the back of the house" and regard a colleague who does it as what we would call a "boot-licker."

Cultural limitations also include appropriate expressions of friendship or liking. An official who wants to build his colleagues' trust in him must make certain kinds of symbolic gestures to express his friendship for them. Thus, a Thai official will frequently treat his colleagues to drinks or to meals and participate in their religious merit-making ceremonies. If he does not, he is likely to be stigmatized as stingy.

Another cultural limitation on role making in organizations is the degree of diffuseness or specificity customary in relations among organizational colleagues. Thai officials customarily engage in social exchange of a much broader range of mutual assistance than we are accustomed to seeing in similar relationships in the United States.

The relationship between the three strategies for creating trust mentioned above (reliance on prior relationships, reliance on professionalism, and reliance on social exchange) and the cultural limitations on social exchange should be clear. Each strategy is employed in a given cultural context, and its use will be governed by specific expectations and norms of conduct. If, to establish trust, one relies on a prior relationship, it will be of a certain named type and will be governed by the expectations customarily attached to this relationship. If one relies on professionalism, then one is limited by the norms of the specific profession as they have been developed in a specific time and place. Even reliance on social exchange without other supports is culturally limited. For, social exchange takes place, not between two random individuals, but between two occupants of named social positions, and there are always cultural prescriptions concerning the types of goods or services that may appropriately be exchanged between occupants of certain positions. With these considerations in mind let us turn now to a more integrated statement of the problem on which this study will focus.

THE RESEARCH PROBLEM

The problem of this research is to investigate some of the ways in which the behavior of Thai district officials and physicians in a provincial hos-

pital is limited, directed, and channeled by certain
structural and cultural features of Thailand and of
the Thai civil service. The structural features to
be examined include: (1) the distribution of various sorts of power among officials, with special
attention given to the effects of (a) centralization
of decision making power, (b) division of responsibility between territorial administrators and technical officials, (c) lack of adequate staff at higher levels to gather and interpret information, (d)
control by certain officials of scarce resources,
(e) the ability of certain officials to deal with
uncertainty by obtaining resources from outside the
organization; (2) the nature of the incentive system with special attention given to (a) the general
inadequacy of official salaries, (b) the uncertainty of reward for good work, (c) the sorts of work or
personal services that are rewarded.

The cultural features to be examined include:
(1) professionalism--the character of Thai medical
professionalism and its effects on physicians' role
making; (2) norms of deference governing interpersonal relations between subordinates and superiors
and among equals; (3) norms governing the expression
of regard and the symbolic means for maintaining
friendship; (4) norms governing prior relationships,
especially graduation from a common university. In
general, this study will attempt to show that the
above structural and cultural factors limit and
channel the behavior of district officials and
provincial physicians into predictable patterns,
that there is considerable uniformity in patterns of
social exchange within each of the two groups, and
that there are predictable differences between them
which can be explained by the structural and cultural factors.

THE DATA

The data on which this analysis is based were
gathered by field observations, by interview, and by
survey questionnaire. Four and a half months were
spent in field observation and interviewing in a
district office and a similar length of time in a
provincial hospital. The incidents and quotations in
the text below are taken from data gathered during
this phase of the research. The district office
studied is referred to by the fictitious name of
"Central District," and the provincial hospital is
called "Riverton Hospital."

Hypotheses drawn from the observational phase

34

of the research were tested by a questionnaire survey of five district offices and five provincial
hospitals. Survey responses were tabulated and the
resulting statistics were analyzed. Discussions in
the following chapters of "the survey" or of "survey
responses" refer to this questionnaire study. A
fuller discription of the methods of data collection
and analysis used in this study is contained in the
Appendix.

THE TRANSLITERATION AND PRONUNCIATION OF THAI WORDS

The following system has been adopted for
transliterating Thai words into Roman script. Vowels
have approximately the values that they have in con-
tinental European languages. The combination "oe" is
used for the central, unrounded vowel in Thai, as in
the word "amp'oe". The sound is similar to that of
the "er" in "her" as it is pronounced in British
standard usage. The combination "ae" represents
roughly the sound of the "a" in the English word
"fact". The symbol "ǫ" is used to represent the central, rounded vowel and has approximately the sound
of the "aw" in the English "saw". The symbol "ṳ"
represents the rear, unrounded vowel, as in the word
"mṳang". It has no European equivalent, but the
sound is that produced by attempting to say "oo"
with the lips formed into a smile. Vowel length and
tone have been disregarded.
The consonants have their familiar English values with a few exceptions. The stǫps "p," "t," and
"k" are unaspirated; the symbol "c̬" is used for the
unvoiced, unaspirated fricative, and "ch" is used
for the aspirated. The letter "j" has the value
given to it in German. The combination "ng" has the
value given to it in the English word "sing" even
when appearing at the beginning of a word. Several
Thai consonants take special pronunciations at the
ends of words, and many written letters are silent.
In this study, words are transliterated as they are
spoken rather than as they are written (e. g.,
"tambon" not "tambol"), except that personal names
are spelled according to the usage of their posses-
sors. For words in current international usage (e.
g., "Bangkok"), the commonly accepted spellings have
been retained.

35

NOTES

1. The help which is offered when we have not asked (but would have liked to) is especially valued for two reasons. First, it is a clearer indication of the helper's regard for us because the help was offered spontaneously rather than under social pressure (See Kelly, 1967, or Hastorf et al., 1970, for the problems of attributing internal causality for the acts of others). Moreover, asking for help places us in the uncomfortable position of having to admit our incapacity to do a job alone (Blau, 1963). It is for these reasons that in extremely unequal, hierarchical relationships like those between landlords and peasants in peasant societies, the peasant is expected to give his services without being asked or may even be ordered to perform them, while the lord waits to be asked. The peasant humbles himself by asking; the lord never **does**. On the other hand, the person who gives too much without being asked is also disliked because he puts us in the uncomfortable position of being saddled with debts which we cannot easily repay or because his favors are seen as directed toward getting something in return rather than as expressions of his regard for us (Jones, 1964).

2. Experimental evidence indicates that people are happiest when they are fairly rewarded. They do not minimize their effort but rather adjust it to the size of the reward. For reviews of this research, see Adams (1965) or Walster et al. (1973)

3. The Distribution of Power at Central District

The distribution of power in the Central District office is one of the principal structural factors which determine patterns of social exchange among its officials. The distribution of power is determined in part by the formal, official division of authority and in part by informal or unintended sources of power which emerge to alter it. One such unintended element in Thai district administration is the ambiguity of the relationship between the technical officials and the district officer. Another unintended source of power of district officials is the lack of staff assistance for the provincial governor combined with extreme centralization of formal authority in his hands. Finally, the power to reward good work by officials is highly centralized and at the same time ambiguously distributed among the administrative generalists, the heads of provincial technical sections, and the heads of departments in the central administration in Bangkok, and this ambiguity provides a broad area for maneuvering by lower officials.

This chapter will take up these aspects of the formal and informal distribution of power at the Central District office and in Northern Province. A full discussion of the rewards and incentives of Thai officials will be taken up in Chapter Four, and these two chapters will provide the background for the analysis of the patterns of social exchange at the district presented in Chapter Five. Before entering into a detailed description of power among the staff of the office of Central District and Northern Province, however, a brief general description of the district may be useful.

CENTRAL DISTRICT

The Central District of Northern Province is
a broad plain covered with rice paddies and dotted
with palm trees and scattered farm houses. The
people there are prosperous as peasants go. Until
recently they lived the relaxed, easy-going life
that gave Thailand its exceptional charm, but now
great changes are taking place. The traveler com-
ing up from Bangkok can see some of them quite
easily from the window of his train. Next to
fields where buffalo make their slow rounds pulling
wooden plows, the traveler can see big disk plows
pulled by Massey-Ferguson tractors. In the grounds
of the temple beyond the paddies, there is a new
school house; perhaps a tall tower for the school's
running water system stands by the ancient pagoda
on which a string of electric lights has been hung.
Next to the railroad track a new Datsun pickup
truck converted to a bus dashes along the red
laterite road carrying people, vegetables and
chickens to market.

Approaching Northtown, the train passes the
province's small airport and next to it the anten-
nas of a military radio-communications station; the
large buildings and spacious grounds of the provincial hospital flash by; as the train slows down,
it passes the storage tanks of an oil company distribution center, and a tall new hotel comes into
view across the roofs of the town just before the
Japanese diesel electric engine brings the train
to a halt in the Northtown station.

Northtown is the capital of Northern Province
which lies on one of the tributaries of the Chao
Phraya River in the northern part of the central
rice plains of Thailand. Northern Province has a
population of about 600,000 and an area of a little
less than 10,000 square kilometers. The economy
of the province is mainly agricultural, and rice
is by far the most important crop. There are also
forestry, fishing, and a few small industries of
which the most important process the province's
agricultural and forest products. Northern Province is moderately wealthy compared to the kingdom as a whole, but for its region it is rich.

Within Northern Province, the distribution of
wealth is quite uneven. Central District has 29.6
percent of the population of the province in only
7.4 percent of its area. This concentration of
population is accompanied by a relatively high

development of business and commercial activity.
Central District, including Northtown, collected
about 40 baht in business tax (a turnover tax on
business volume) per capita of population in 1973,
while the province as a whole collected only 14
baht per capita. Northtown is the province's only
incorporated municipality.

The relatively high level of development of
Central District in comparison to the outlying districts is important in determining the character of
official activity for two principal reasons. First,
the wealth of the district, and especially of
Northtown, provides relatively large resources of
development projects in the rural parts of the district. These resources are tapped by the district
officials in unofficial ways and applied to development projects in the district as will be discussed
in more detail in Chapter Five. The other important consequence of the relatively high level of
development of Central District is that its people
make relatively heavy demands on the district's
staff. The small size and extensive road network
of Central District make it easier than in other
districts for peasants to go to the district office.
At the same time, merchants often have business at
their district office, and since there are many
more merchants in Northtown than in the province's
other district capitals, Central District is a busy
place. As we shall see, the effect of these factors is to intensify social exchange among the district officials. The extra resources make it possible for them to do more development work, and the
extra demands of citizens increase the dependence
of officials on one another. So, the whole cycle
of social exchange among officials and between
officials and citizens becomes more rapid and in-
tense.

THE ORGANIZATION OF CENTRAL DISTRICT OFFICE

The office of Central District is a medium
sized, two story wooden building with a circular
drive and an attractive lawn in front. Indeed, except for the large number of glass-less windows and
the crowds of people going in and out, it looks not
unlike a fifty year old suburban house in the
american midwest. Inside is a large room that fills
the entire lower floor of the building and that is
divided into work areas by counters of slightly
less than chest height. Each of the areas is used

FIGURE 3.1

SIMPLIFIED ORGANIZATIONAL CHART OF CENTRAL DISTRICT

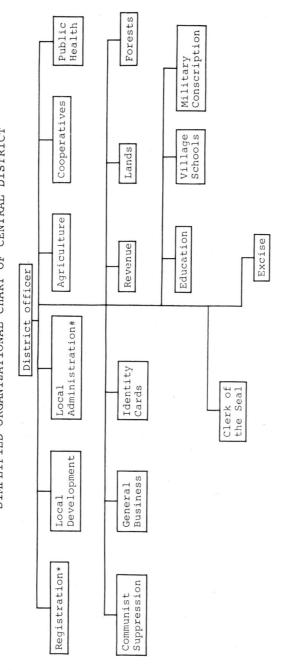

*Officials of the Local Administration Section are shown on the left hand side of the chart, and officials of the other sections are shown at the right.

#One of the deputy district officers is said to be in charge of "Local Administration." This means that certain routine administrative chores like singing land titles or marriage certificates are delegated to hom and that in emergencies when the district officer is not present this deputy acts for him. However, the designation of one deputy in this way does not imply that the other deputies are not members of the Local Administration Section. All of the officials listed on the left hand side of the chart are members of that section.

40

by one of the sections of the district administration. In the center of the room, directly opposite
the entrance, is a stairway to the second floor
which consists of two rooms. One is a large room
divided into sections like the ones downstairs, and
the other is the office of the district officer. It
is reached through a pair of glass doors through
which the visitor may see him hard at work signing
orders, listening to problems brought by villagers,
or conferring with his staff.

The Local Administration Section

The district officer's staff includes two
classes of officials. First, there are the deputy
district officers (palad amp'oe) and the clerk of
the seal (samiantra). They belong, as the district
officer does, to the Department of Local Administration of the Ministry of the Interior, and some of
them hope to be district officers themselves one
day. They assist the district officer to carry out
the policies and programs of the department and to
supervise the heads of the other sections of the
district administration.

The deputy district officers, of whom there
are six at Central District, the look of the seal
and several clerks form the Local Administration
Section. The work of this section is of three main
sorts. First, the section maintains the registration files. Every resident of Thailand must be
registered in a household. The household register
is the basic list on which the other files depend.
To get a passport or a driver's license, to enter
school, or to register for military conscription,
one must show his household registration. In addition, every citizen over the age of seventeen
must have an identity card, and the district officials are responsible for issuing these. Besides
these basic registers, there are the marriage
register, the register of births and deaths, the
register of draft animals, the registers of various
kinds of businesses, and the gun register.

The officials who keep the registers are also
responsible for issuing permits to engage in various regulated activities. For example, one must
obtain and renew annually permits to engage in most
businesses. In short, virtually every citizen of
Central District has many occasions in his life to
do business at the Local Administration Section of
the district office. The officials there can

expedite or obstruct a person's business as the occasion or personal inclination dictate, and we shall see that they use this power to encourage people to cooperate with the district's development programs.

The second major aspect of the work of the Local Administration Section is the arbitration of disputes among citizens. When villagers have legal disputes, they often go to the district officer for arbitration rather than to court for a trial because the latter is expensive and uncertain. However, the district officer could not possibly arbitrate all of the villagers' disputes himself; so he usually delegates the duty to his deputies.

The third major sort of work that the Local Administration officials do is to promote projects of local development. Each year the district collects from the villagers a small land tax known as the Local Development Tax (p'asi bamrung t'ǫngt'i), and the money is used for local development projects of which the most important are roads to connect the villages to each other and to the district capital.[1] The development program is important to the district officials, and it has led to great changes in their relationships with the villagers.

The officials have found that they cannot carry out the local development program without the cooperation of the villagers, and that cooperation is much easier to obtain if the villagers are reasonably democratically involved in planning development projects. Moreover, the villagers' interest in local development has grown over the years as they have seen its favorable effects. Meksawan (1961:238-42) reported that Thai villagers were initially rather apathetic about building roads because they could not see their value for people like themselves who walked everywhere. Now, however, they have had a chance to see that as soon as a road reaches a village, someone buys a truck and uses it to operate a bus service. Then, it is no longer necessary to walk, and everyone can see the advantage of that.

At the same time, the villagers can easily see that their cooperation in building roads is urgently desired by the officials of the district whose careers depend in part on their success in promoting development. So, the villagers are in a position to trade their cooperation for other sorts of assistance from officials. To put it differently,

42

the villagers want the roads, but they know that if
they do not appear too eager for them, they can get
something in return for their cooperation.[2] This
is important because, as we shall see, a great deal
of the social exchange at the district centers
around the problem of obtaining citizens' cooperation in local development.

The Other Sections

        In addition to Local Administration, there are
a number of other sections, each of which is staffed
by a section head and one or more clerks. The sections are:

        Revenue (samubanchi)
        Excise (samp'asamit)
        Lands (t'idin)
        Forests (pa maj)
        Public Health (anamaj)
        Village Schools (muad kansuksa)
        Education (suksat'ikan)
        Agricultural Extension (kaset)
        Cooperatives (sahakon)
        Military Conscription (sasdi)

        Figure 3.1 shows the administrative organiza-
tion of Central District. It shows that in principle all authority rests with the district officer although in practice the situation is somewhat
more complex than that, as the next section will
show.

THE POWER OF THE DISTRICT OFFICER

        The district officer supervises and coordi-
nates the work of the officials of the district, but
his relationship with them is somewhat different
from what the reader familiar with american administrative practice might expect. Our orientation is
technical, and our administrative tradition stresses
decentralization. Therefore, we give the technical
official a great of independence to do his work as
he sees fit while providing him with general administrative guidelines, and in order to permit administrative control, we have developed elaborate
techniques for evaluation and reporting.
        The Thai orientation is not technical but
paternalistic, and the administrative tradition is
one in which power is closely held at the center

43

(Siffin, 1966:166). The Thais therefore give the
technical official very little independent authority. Instead, it is held by a generalist who takes
a fatherly responsibility for his people, and the
technical roles are defined as advisory. In practice, this means that a great many minor matters
which would be handled by the sections in an American organization are submitted to the district officer for his approval in Thailand. For example,
a section head must get the district officer's approval to go into the field to work; any expenditure of funds, no matter how small, must be approved by the district officer, and so on.

Of course, the district officer cannot really
supervise the work of his subordinates as closely
as his official responsibilities appear to require,
and if he tried to do so the work of the district
would rapidly grind to a halt. The amount of real
supervision he exercises over a section depends on
his interest in its work, on the limits of his
technical expertise,and on his trust in the section
chief. The district officer supervises very
closely the work of the Local Administration Section because it is his section in a way that the
others are not. His own superiors in the Department of Local Administration rate his work primarily on his success in promoting the department's
own programs. So, he in turn keeps close watch on
the work of his deputies.

The heads of the technical sections have somewhat more autonomy. This is partly because the
district officer, being a generalist, is not expert
in the technical specialities of his subordinates
and therefore must ordinarily accept their recommendations. He will try to be sure that their recommendations are not contrary to laws or regulations or to national, provincial, or district
policies, and he will interest himself in all personnel matters. But ordinarily he will not question the technical aspects of a section's work unless he does not trust the section head.

Moreover, the technical officials at the district have technical superiors at the provincial
level, and they and the district officer share
power over the district's technical workers. The
division of authority between the technical superiors and the district officer is ambiguous, and
he must try to maintain good relations with them
in order to be able to control his own subordinates.
Even if good relations are maintained, his control

is problematic.

Another reason for the limited ability of the district officer to supervise closely the work of his subordinates is that he has an extraordinarily heavy work load. In a busy district, he may work fourteen hours a day including weekends. He has a great deal of office work to do; he must consider and approve the proposals of his subordinates, and if he slows down, the whole district will slow down with him because nothing can be done without his approval. In addition, his fatherly responsibility for the welfare of his people and the success of the local development program require him to spend a great deal of time in the field.

An example of the district officer's "fatherly responsibility" may give the reader a clearer idea of what it means. I once spent the whole of one Saturday with the district officer of Central District as he walked the length of a long drainage canal to persuade the villagers to remove the dams they had put up as fish traps. The fish traps had caused the water in the rice fields drained by the canal to remain the the fields longer than it should have, and the farmers were unable to harvest their rice in the standing water. So they had appealed to the district officer to solve their problem. He could have ordered the police to deal with it, but he did not do so. Instead, he went personally on a weekend to persuade the villagers to remove their traps. He made it quite clear, however, that he meant to be obeyed. He said that if the traps were not removed by the next day, the police would be ordered to take action. He gave the villagers a choice: they could comply voluntarily and save their equipment, or they could let the police confiscate it. This personal way of dealing with village problems is a regular feature of the district officer's job. It is normatively expected, and in addition he could not possibly enlist the villagers' cooperation in development if he made a regular practice of turning them over without warning to the tender mercies of the police.

The district officer also has a ceremonial role. He must be present at official openings of new facilities, and he must attend the religious, merit making ceremonies of his subordinates and of other important people like village headmen. If the district officer failed to play his ceremonial role well, the district's effectiveness would

45

surely suffer. This is because attendance at a ceremony expresses the district officer's concern for the people giving it; it tells them that he will be willing to help them when they need help, and this assurance makes them more willing to help the district with its work. Therefore the district officer would not think of stinting his ceremonial obligations, although he frequently complains of the time they take up. Thus, the district officer has a very heavy work load which prevents him from supervising closely the work of his technical subordinates. He must trust them to do good work most of the time.

A final limitation on the district officer's power over his subordinates is his lack of control of the rewards they receive. As this will be discussed more fully in the next chapter, it will only be alluded to here. The district officer cannot consistently reward his subordinates with salary raises or advancement. He can only recommend rewards.[3] His recommendations must pass the provincial section heads and the governor before being sent to the departments in Bangkok for the final decision. At each level, recommendations may be altered; so the district officer's power is limited by his inability to control the behavior of provincial and departmental officials in rewarding their subordinates in his district.

Therefore, the district officer's real ability to compel the obedience of his technical staff is limited. His power over the deputy district officers is greater, and he spends more time supervising them, but even they may to some degree elude his control by cultivating powerful friends further up in the hierarchy. So, the district officer must trust his subordinates to considerable degree if any work is to be done, and he must try through social exchange to build their trust and their loyalty to him in order to get them to put their best efforts into their work.

THE DISTRICT IN THE NATIONAL ADMINISTRATIVE
  STRUCTURE

Central District is the end of a complex chain of command which reaches from the ministries in Bangkok through the provincial headquarters, and in order to understand the distribution of power in the district office, one must know something of its relationships to units higher up the chain. It

46

is organized into three levels: the central administration, the province, and the district.

The central administration includes the ministries, departments, divisions, and sections in the capital. From the perspective of the district officials, the most important level of the central administration is the department. Each major substantive area of work is organized into a department, and each department is represented by a section (p'anaek) at the province and again at the district.[4] Each civil official belongs to a certain department. He wears a brass medal on the collar of his uniform which identifies the department to which he belongs and within which he spends most of his working life. Transfers from one department to another are not unknown, but they are rare (Siffin, 1966:173). Orders to the province usually come in the name of the director-general of a department, and all recommendations concerning promotions, salary increases, or transfer of officials must be approved by the directors-general of their respective departments.

Between the central administration and the district is the province (čanqwat). Each province is headed by a governor (p'uwarachakan čanqwat) who carries the full responsibility for the administration of his province just as the district officer does in his district. Under the governor are the various provincial section chiefs who represent the departments that have operations in the province. They advise the governor concerning their areas of technical expertise and carry out the policies of the governor and of their respective departments. Like their counterparts at the district, the provincial section heads can do little without the formal approval of the governor. In Northern Province, for example, a provincial section chief could approve the expenditure of no more than 2000 baht (about 100) at a time; for larger amounts, the approval of the governor was required.

The governor is limited in his control over his section heads just as the district officer is by his lack of technical expertise, by the size of his work load, and by the division of responsibility between generalists and technical specialists. However, the governor is limited even further by his lack of an advisory staff. A province is a big unit compared to a district, and a governor cannot possibly keep abreast by himself of the field work of all of the officials under him. Indeed, the load of paperwork that the centralization of authority in his hands requires him to carry makes it difficult for him to know all that goes on in the provincial offices. If he had an advisory staff to report on conditions in the field and to review proposals from the sections, he would be able to supervise them more closely but he does not have such a staff.

In principle, the section heads are supposed to serve as the governor's advisory staff, but in practice their duties as line administrators leave them little time for advisory duties. Moreover, the division of authority between generalists and technical specialists that weakened the district officer is repeated at the provincial level. Just as the district's technicians can play the district officer off against their provincial superiors, so the latter can play the governor off against their superiors in the central administration. The power to reward good work lies ultimately with the department heads in the central administration, and consequently the loyalty of the provincial officials to the governor is not unlimited.[5]

Therefore, the section heads cannot be regarded as an adequate staff, and thus the governor has no real advisory staff composed of officials without line responsibility and loyal to him. Lacking such a staff and carrying a tremendous load of paperwork, the governor cannot keep himself informed of the progress of work in the field except in emergencies. He can trouble-shoot, but he cannot really supervise. One thing the governor can do is to render his section heads' work convenient and speedy or exasperatingly slow. He must approve all programs and expenditures and can delay or expedite things at will. This provides some incentive for subordinates to be trustworthy and loyal because one who is will find that his requests are speedily granted while a disloyal or untrustworthy subordinate will find that his requests are slowly and carefully scrutinized.

The governor's lack of a staff to help him keep informed has important consequences in the behavior of district officials. They can exploit the fact that the governor will be grateful to anyone who visits him occasionally with reliable information. By so doing, they can bring themselves to his notice in a legitimate way and so improve their chances of advancement. The same is true to a lesser degree of district officials' relations with their provincial section chiefs.

Figure 3.2

SIMPLIFIED CHART OF THE STRUCTURE OF THE
TERRITORIAL ADMINISTRATION OF THAILAND

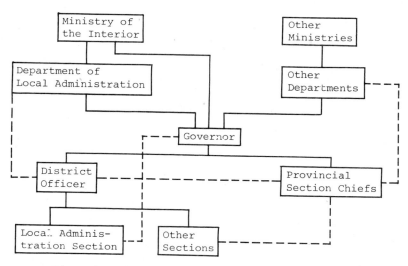

————— Line of official, administrative authority.

— — — Line of informal authority and communication.

The relationships among the central administration, the province, and the district are shown
in Chart 2. In principle, the district section
heads are subordinate to the district officer, and
he in turn is subordinate to the governor. The
governor has technical subordinates who advise him
on the programs and policies of their respective
departments. Orders from the province to the district, however, are always from the governor to
the district officer--never from a provincial section head to a district section head. Likewise,
reports from the district to the province are always from the district officer to the governor.
Communications from any central ministry come to
the governor and are passed on by him to the appropriate section heads. At least, that is the
official picture.
In fact, of course, there is a continual communication between the district section heads and
their respective provincial superiors and between

the provincial section heads and their superiors in
Bangkok. A district technical official will usually
consult with his provincial superior before sub-
mitting a proposal to the district officer for his
approval, and a provincial section head will want
to make sure that he knows about conditions in the
districts before proposing anything important to
the governor. Moreover, a good provincial section
chief will have friends in his department on whom
he can rely to help him get funds for his work. The
district officer, being equal in rank to a provincial section head, has his own line of informal
communication with his superiors in Bangkok. Figure
3.2 summarizes this discussion. The figure also
shows the ambiguity of the division of authority
between the generalists and the technicians. Both
the flow of information and the power to reward or
punish subordinates follow the informal lines of
authority and communication as much as the formal
lines. So, an official who wishes to advance in
his career must build relations with his superiors
in both systems.

THE POWER OF SUBORDINATE OFFICIALS

     It should be clear from the above discussion
that the ambiguities and conflicts in the distribution of power among the various levels of the
territorial administration of Thailand provide
ample opportunity for an enterprising junior official to increase his power relative to that of any
particular superior. The reader should understand,
however, what is meant by this: power, as this study
is using the term, refers to the inverse of dependence. Hence, as the dependence of one official on
another decreases, the power of the former relative
to that of the latter increases. Thus, for example,
a district official may, by assiduously cultivating
his relations with his provincial superior, increase
his power relative to the district officer. The
subordinate may accomplish this by exploiting his
provincial superior's need for information or in
other ways as will be discussed in Chapter Five.
     Another important source of power of subordi-
nates which will be discussed in detail in Chapter
Five is the subordinate's access to resources
needed by the district for its work. Certain officials are able to obtain resources because in the
course of their work they are able to place citizens
under social obligations. That is, such officials
may do favors for citizens and therefore be in a

position to ask for favors in return. The ability
to obtain resources in this manner is used in social
exchange in ways which will be discussed later. At
this point, however, we should note that the power
to obtain resources in not equally distributed among
the district's officials. Some can get quite a lot
while others are able to obtain less. Those who can
obtain more can use the resources they control in
building their relationships both with their colleagues and with their superiors.

VILLAGE ADMINISTRATION

The district is the lowest level of the regular
territorial administration, but below the district
there is a kind of semirepresentative and semi-
administrative village government. Within each district there are a number of villages, and each of
these has an elected headman (p'ujajban). The villages are grouped in communes (tambon), and the
head of a commune is called a kamnan. He is elected
by the people of his commune from among the headmen
of its villages.
The kamnan and the headmen are responsible
directly to the district officer. He can remove
them from office for corruption or incompetence,
although he rarely does so. This means that the
district officer controls official access to the
villages and he can facilitate or obstruct the work
of any other official there. This is an important
source of power for him, and he uses it to obtain
the cooperation of other officials and agencies with
his policies.
This completes the description of the organization of the district and its place in the national
administrative structure. The description has been
deliberately simplified; some things have been left
out because discussion of them would add nothing
to the reader's understanding of the problems to
which this study addresses itself. Thus, for
example, no attention has been given to incorporated
units of local government because they are not
important determinants of district officials' behavior. The regional level of the territorial administration has also been ignored and for the same
reason. There are also some departments that have
field units which function independently of the
province or the district. The Irrigation Department
and the Accelerated Rural Development Program are
examples. These are relevant to this study only as

51

parts of the environment within which the district works. As such, they have a role to play, and it will be discussed later on, but a consideration of their internal structures would take us too far afield.

CONCLUSIONS

This chapter has given a general description of Central District, of the structure of its staff and of its organizational context. One important aspect of this structure is the distribution of power in the district and provincial organizations. It is characterized by a high degree of centralization of formal authority combined with a lack of supervisory capability. There is also a high degree of ambiguity in the relationship between the administrative generalists who govern territorial units and the technical specialists responsible for specific sorts of programs. The lack of advisory staff at the provincial level is also important because it provides opportunities for district officials to build relation with their provincial superiors by acting as informal sources of information. In addition, the centralization of reward power serves to weaken the district officer and to complicate the problems of officials in obtaining advancement as will be discussed in Chapter Five.

The sources of power of subordinates were also briefly discussed. Subordinates' power was said to derive from three sources which are: (1) the ambiguity in the generalist-specialist relationship, (2) the use of the ability to supply scarce information to "go over one's superior's head" to the next higher level, and (3) informal access to resources needed by the district in its work.

Finally, mention was made of the district officer's very powerful position in relation to the village level of administration and of the fact that he can use his monopoly of entry into the villages of his district to obtain favors from other officials or official agencies. This description of the distribution of power in the district office and its organizational setting has partly set the stage for the description of role making by district officials. I turn now to a discussion of the other important structural determinant of official social exchange which is the system of incentives and rewards.

NOTES

1. Actually, only 80% of the money is used
for projects. The other 20% is used for administrative costs at the provincial and district
levels.

2. The villagers' desire for roads and other
sorts of development was evident both from conversations with them and from their willingness to
give pieces of their land for such projects. I do
not know how conscious or deliberate the peasants'
behavior was in concealing their interest in development. However, there can be no doubt that the
exchanges between villagers and officials that are
described in Chapter Five took place, and it seems
implausible that the villagers were completely unaware of what they were doing.

3. He can order some minor punishments, but
this power is rarely used. An examination of the
records of Central District revealed no instance of
disciplinary action during the previous five years,
and only two cases of officials who were transferred to other posts either because they failed
to do their work properly or because they were
unable to get along with the district officer.

4. The word "section" is used for three quite
different sorts of units in the Thai bureaucracy.
In the central administration, a section is the
unit below a division and is headed by a second
grade official. In the provincial administration,
a section (also known as a "suan rachakan" is the
functional unit directly below the governor and is
headed by a first grade official. At the district,
the section is the unit directly below the district
officer and is headed by a second or a third grade
official.

5. The governor has even less power to punish
subordinates at the level of provincial section
chief than to reward them. The governor cannot
even transfer an official at this level to a new
post. He can, of course, find informal ways of
making a section chief's life difficult as is
discussed in the text.

4. Incentives in the Civil Service

In order to explain the behavior of Thai
officials we must know something of the rewards
for which they work, both formal and informal.
The formal rewards consist of advancement in grade
and salary, and these are contingent on the quality
of an official's work, on his seniority and, as we
shall see, on some other things as well. Informal
rewards include prestige, autonomy in doing one's
work, illicit income from various sources, the
satisfaction that comes from public service, and
the security of a civil service career. Of these,
prestige, autonomy, and illicit income are contingent on advancement and hence to be obtained in
part by the same means. Security and satisfaction
are unrelated to advancement.

FORMAL INCENTIVES

The Structure of Grades and Positions

Every Thai official has a grade which is comparable to a rank in the army. There are five
grades which are in ascending order the fourth,
third, second, first, and special grades.[1] The
fourth grade is the entry level for officials without university degrees. Fourth grade officials are
recruited locally in each province by competitive
examination. Candidates must have secondary school
(M.S. 3[2]) certificates. Fourth grade officials
hold a variety of positions, but ordinarily do not
have administrative responsibility.

The third grade is the lowest commissioned
(sanjabat) grade, and it is the entry level for
officials with bachelor's degrees. At the district
office, third grade officials are heads of sections

and deputy district officers. Above the third grade is the second grade which is the entry level for officials with master's degrees. Second grade officials at the district office perform duties similar to those of third grade officials. However, the grade required for occupancy of a given position is always specified, and a third grade official may not ordinarily hold a second grade position, nor may a second grade official be appointed to a third grade position. When an official has qualifications which make him especially suitable for a particular position but does not have a high enough grade, he may be assigned as the acting tenant of the position. He may not be promoted to the higher grade on the basis of his skills or accomplishments unless he has sufficient seniority and has passed the required competitive examination.

The second and third grades correspond to what we would call middle management positions in the provincial and district hierarchy. Officials of these grades have some authority to supervise subordinates and to plan and work independently. Indeed, as we have discussed, some of them have a good deal of independence. But they are definitely not high officials. The first and special grades are top management. At the district there is only one first grade official, the district officer, and at the provincial office the section chiefs are usually first grade officials. Special grade officials are appointed by the king, and in the provincial administration, only the governor and the assistant governor, if there is one, are of the special grade.

Advancement Through the Grades

Within each grade there are a number of salary steps, and an official ordinarily receives a raise in salary of one step each year. When he reaches a certain salary level, he becomes eligible to take the examination[3] for promotion to the next higher grade. If he passes the examination, he is eligible for promotion, but he cannot be promoted unless there is a position vacant at the higher grade. If no such position is available, the official's name is put on a list of those eligible for promotion. If he fails to be promoted within two years, he must take the examination again, and it is not uncommon for officials to pass the promotional examinations more than once.

The various departments use different rules to decide who will be promoted from among those who have passed a promotional examination. In some departments, the candidate with the highest examination score is promoted first, and in some departments the most senior candidate or the candidate with the highest salary is promoted first. In many departments, it appears that personal recommendations from high officials play a role in decisions about who is to be promoted. Discussion with district officials revealed that the various departments were not uniform in this regard, however. Some departments were believed by their members to be quite impartial in making decisions about promotions while other departments appeared to be governed mainly by patronage.

This variation among departments should not surprise us. Several researchers have noted that in Thai administration the personal inclinations of high level officials are more important than the regulations of the Thai civil service might seem to allow. Impartial rules are not always impartially enforced, and what Siffin (1966:163) called the "override" is quite common.

An official who does exceptionally good work in a particular year may have his salary increased by two steps. A person who receives frequent double raises of this sort not only obtains a higher salary than his less fortunate contemporaries but also advances faster because he becomes eligible to take the examination for promotion to the next grade sooner than a person who receives few double raises. So, getting double raises is the key to advancement.

Officials seek advancement in any organization, but in the Thai civil service advancement is particularly important because of the inadequacy of salaries in the lower grades. A study by the Civil Service Commission of Thailand indicated that the salaries of officials were smaller than their expenses in every grade below the first grade (Sawasdi and Wachiraworakara, 1973), even when the fringe benefits to which officials were entitled were included in the analysis. The data for this study were gathered in 1971, and since then the rate of inflation has been a good deal greater than the rate of increase in the salaries of officials.

However, while everyone strives for double raises, they are few and far between for most district officials. At the time of this research

(1973-5), the rule was that no more than 10 percent of the fourth and third grade officials in the kingdom nor more than 6 percent of the second and first grade officials could receive double raises in one year. Thus, an official could in principle go for more than ten years without a double raise even if his work were quite good.

Another reason for the difficulty experienced by many officials in getting double raises is that the system of evaluation of officials' work is extremely cumbersome and unstandardized, while at the same time, the decisions to give double raises are made by high level superiors who are distant from the field and have little opportunity to see what their subordinates are doing. This combination virtually eliminates the possibility of giving double raises fairly or impartially.

The method of evaluation is that each official writes a report of what he has done during the preceding year.[4] He paints his accomplishments in the brightest possible colors, but inevitably some officials are better writers than others. Moreover, some kinds of work lend themselves better to dramatic presentation than others. For example, an official who has built a road can describe the road. He can list in impressive detail the voluntary contributions of the villagers and show how much money his skill in eliciting contributions has saved the state. He can include a photograph of happy villagers working on the road, and a photograph of the governor making a speech at the ceremony inaugurating its use. In contrast, an official in charge of household registrations may have worked very hard to provide the best possible service to the villagers who come to his section. He may have put in a great deal of overtime signing documents in order to reduce the time the villagers had to wait for them. But what can he say in his report?

If the decision to grant him a double raise were made by his immediate superior who had a chance to see him at work, this obstacle might not be quite so large, but in fact the district officer cannot grant a double raise to a subordinate. He can only recommend to the governor that a double raise should be awarded to a certain official. Moreover, the governor does not receive the district officer's recommendation directly. Before the governor sees the recommendation, it must be sent to the official's provincial section chief who makes recommendations concerning his subordinates both at the province and at the district.[5]

Thus, for example, the provincial agricultural extension officer receives the recommendations of all of the district officers concerning district agricultural extension officers. The provincial agricultural officer, who has few occasions to visit even Central District and rarely goes to the outlying districts, must decide whom to recommend for a double raise. The number of double raises that can be given is small. So, he cannot support several recommendations for double raises in the districts. Moreover, he has subordinates in his own office to consider. Their work is right in front of his eyes, and he is made daily aware of the difficulties that they face in accomplishing their tasks. So, he is much more likely to be appreciative of their contributions than of those of the distant district officials. So, a district official who has done good work is much less likely to be rewarded with a double raise than is a provincial official who has done good work unless the former has contrived ways to bring his accomplishments to the personal attention of his provincial superior.

When the standards of evaluation are so vague, there is a great deal of opportunity for favoritism. Therefore, officials seek occasions to maintain personal contact with their superiors in order to earn their favor. Naturally, officials who are physically close to the provincial offices have a considerable advantage in this respect, because they can visit their provincial superiors often, while the officials of distant districts must limit the number of their visits to the provincial capital. The apparent effect of these factors, at least in Northern Province, is that a disproportionately large number of double raises are given to the officials stationed in Northtown, either in the provincial office or in Central District office as is shown in Table 4.1. The advantage accruing to officials in Northtown testifies to the importance of personal contact with superiors in obtaining advancement in the Thai civil service.

It should be noted that the disadvantage of being in an outlying district is far greater for fourth grade officials than for the other grades. This is consistent with my contention that the reason for the disparity is that officials of outlying districts have greater difficulty in building

TABLE 4.1

Advantage of Officials Stationed in Northtown Over Officials
Stationed in the Outer Districts in Receiving Double Raises
by Grade from 1969 to 1973

	Grade			
	First	Second	Third	Fourth
(A) Percent of officials in Northern Province who were stationed in:				
Northtown	59	45	36	28
Outer Districts	41	55	64	72
(B) Percent of Double Raises Given in Northern Province that were received by officials stationed in:				
Northtown	77	60	43	65
Outer Districts	23	40	57	35
Ratio of (B) to (A) for:				
Northtown	1.31	1.33	1.19	2.32
Outer Districts	.56	.72	.89	.49

good personal relations with provincial superiors.
Officials of the commissioned grades carry administrative responsibility which gives them at least
some occasions to visit the provincial capital on
official business. Fourth grade officials, in contrast, are almost all clerks and therefore rarely
have occasions to visit the provincial capital.
Consequently, it is extremely difficult for them to
compete with the clerks who work immediately under
the eyes of the provincial section chiefs.

An alternative interpretation of the advantage
enjoyed by officials of the provincial center is
that their superiority accounts for their being rewarded more frequently. While we cannot dismiss
this possibility entirely, it does not seem likely.
During the period of the research, no respondent
mentioned such a practice. What does appear to
happen is that officials who have succeeded in
establishing good personal relations with their
superiors are given posts that maximize their

opportunities for advancement. Such posts may provide opportunities for dramatic achievements or they may simply be close to the superiors.

The importance of personal contact with superiors does not end at the level of the provincial section chief. For he, like the district officer, can only recommend choices to the governor who is inevitably even less well informed than the section chief about the work of his subordinates. Even the governor can only make recommendations to the directors-general of the various departments who must choose whom to promote from among the recommendations of governors throughout the kingdom. The directors-general usually assign to each governor a quota of double raises to award to low level officials, although a governor's decision may be overturned, but when it comes to first and second grade officials, the directors-general reserve to themselves the power to reward their subordinates as they choose. We should find therefore that personal relations with the director-general of one's department or with his immediate subordinates are important in securing advancement. Evidence supporting this is the disproportionately small number of double raises awarded to officials in the provinces compared to those awarded to officials in the offices of the departments in Bangkok.

Lacking data for the whole kingdom, it is difficult to be sure about this, but it is at least true that the proportion of double raises awarded to first and second grade officials in Northern Province was less than for the kingdom as a whole between 1969 and 1973. During that period, 6 percent of the first and second grade officials in the kingdom received double raises, in each year, but in Northern Province only about 4 percent of these grades received double raises[6], which suggests that the assumption of bias in favor of the center is at least plausible. Certainly, the officials believed it existed.

In sum, the situation that faces the Thai district official who wishes to obtain advancement is that advancement is obtained by getting double raises for good work, but the system used for evaluating the work is cumbersome and unstandardized to a degree that makes it extremely difficult to compare the work of one official to that of another. So, work of a very dramatic sort and the ability to write reports well give an official an advantage over his colleagues. At the same time, the centralization of power to reward good work renders it impossible for the official who has to decide whom to reward to overcome by personal observation the inadequacies of the formal evaluation system. Consequently, good work cannot be consistently rewarded, and an official who wishes to advance must contrive to bring himself personally to the notice of his superiors at various levels in order to be recommended and chosen for double raises. The ways in which Thai officials accomplish this will be discussed in the next chapter.

Fringe Benefits

In addition to his regular salary, a Thai official may also receive fringe benefits of various kinds. These function as incentives because the amounts which a person can receive are related to his official grade. Fringe benefits include an official housing allowance, free medical care, and small amounts for the education of officials' children.

In addition to the regular benefits, a high official may also have an official car. In principle, he is supposed to use it only for official business, but in fact the use of official cars as personal transportation is virtually universal. The incentive value of an official car should not be underestimated. The import duty on automobiles is 180 percent of the price. So, a car is equivalent to a very handsome addition to an official's salary.

Officials are also entitled to collect per diem and travel costs whenever they go in the field for more than twelve hours on one trip. Generally, the per diem and travel cost allowances are not sufficient to cover the expenses incurred in going into the field, but they are better than nothing and the officials have to go into the field in any case.

The combined fringe benefits and travel expense allowances can amount to a large proportion of a district official's income. For the deputy district officers at Central District, they equaled between 32 and 42 percent of their salaries during the year before this research was done. None of these officers had cars, but if they had had them, the value of their fringe benefits would have been much greater.

INFORMAL INCENTIVES

Civil service salaries and fringe benefits are quite low. Indeed, Blaug (1971) estimates them to be as low as one-fourth of those paid in private business. Nevertheless, the civil service continues to be by far the most popular career among educated Thai, as can be seen in a study by the National Institute of Development Administration (NIDA, 1972).

NIDA asked all those who applied to enter its graduate school in 1970 what employment they hoped to get after graduation. Of the students who were applying to all of the departments of the Institute, 70 percent hoped to work for the civil service, and 83 percent hoped to work for the state in some capacity. Only 8 percent hoped to work for private businesses. Even among students applying to the Department of Business Administration, 64 percent hoped to work for the state, and only 25 percent for private business. Thus, in spite of the obvious inferiority of official salaries to those paid in private business, educated Thai continue to prefer the civil service to other types of employment. The civil service must therefore offer other sorts of rewards, and to these we now turn our consideration.

Officials responding to the survey were given a list of items that had been mentioned by interview respondents as reasons for preferring the civil service to other careers. Each survey respondent was asked to choose from the list the reason which was most important, second most important, and third most important to him. The responses are shown in Table 4.2. Clearly, the most important informal reward is the financial security offered by the civil service. The salaries are not high, but an official who does not get into trouble is never laid off, and the practice of giving one step raise each year to everyone, regardless of the quality of his work, guarantees a modicum of advancement.

Previous research on Thailand indicates that in general security is an important motive of Thai people. Piker (1968) argues that Thai peasants are caught in an odd sort of bind as a result of the way they are socialized. They like independence, but they are taught not to have much trust in their own abilities. Lacking trust in themselves, they like being dependent on others, but at the same

62

TABLE 4.2
Reasons for Preferring the Civil Service to Other Careers: District Officials

	Percentage of District Officials Saying That a Reason Was for Them:			Percentage Choosing Each Reason as Either (A), (B), or (C)
	(A) Most Important	(B) 2nd Most Important	(C) 3rd Most Important	
The civil service offers great security.	47*	11	10	68
The civil service offers good fringe benefits.	9	33	18	59
The civil service gives me a chance to use my knowledge and skill.	16	10	14	41
I had no money to invest in a private business.	16	10	14	41
The civil service offers opportunity for advancement.	3	19	15	37
Society accords high prestige to a civil servant.	6	8	14	28
I didn't know what else to do.	-	6	9	15

*The columns do not total to 100% because items chosen by very few respondents have been omitted. The right hand column totals to more than 100% because each respondent made three ranked choices.

time they can see for themselves that others are
often not very trustworthy. For a person with
these attitudes, an impersonal organization that
guarantees to support him for life in return for a
moderate amount of work is a perfect solution to
his dilemma.

In addition to security, the civil service
also offers autonomy to these who reach at least
moderately high rank. Several section chiefs at
Central District spoke of the autonomy that their
positions allowed them as pleasing or rewarding.
The importance of this incentive is seen in the
percentage of the respondents who said that they
liked the civil service because it offered them
the chance to use their knowledge and skills.
Many jobs in a district office require a great deal
of knowledge and skill, and the exercise of technical expertise in work has long been recognized
as rewarding because of the sense of mastery it
gives and because of the flattering self concept
it provides.

The achievement of autonomy depends heavily
on the building of one's superior's trust, especially in Thailand. We have seen that officially
a district section head has very little autonomy.
In principle, he works entirely according to the
district officer's orders. However the district
officer is very busy, and it is difficult for him
to supervise the work of his subordinates closely.
Therefore, he is glad to accord a measure of the
practical autonomy to a section head if he believes the man to be trustworthy. The ways that
officials build the district officer's trust will
be discussed in the next chapter.

The civil service also offers its officials a
great deal of prestige. It is an honorable service
which occupies a unique position in the society of
which it is a part. This position is the result of
the long historical development which has been
described briefly in Chapter One above. The consequence of that development was that prior to the
turn of this century, Thailand had a very simple
and unified social structure. There was no independent landed class and no commercial class. So,
power, wealth and prestige were all concentrated
in the royal service.

Much of this has changed. Today, a growing
commercial class competes for status with the
officials, and a modern police force and judiciary
have taken over much of the power of the

administrative generalists. Moreover, the standards by which status is judged are changing. In
the past, land was plentiful while labor was scarce.
Money meant little; for, there was little to buy in
rural Thailand. Wealth and power meant the ability
to command men, and this ability was guaranteed to
Thai officials by the system of corvée (Rabibhadana,
1969:85). Consequently, the status of officials
had a secure foundation. Today, there is no corvée,
and wealth means the possession of money. Officials
are paid salaries, but they are small compared with
the earnings of persons in private business. Wealth
and power are no longer firmly anchored to official
position, and consequently the status of officials
is insecure.

However, these changes are very recent, and
their full effects have not yet been felt. In the
countryside, where the officials of Central District
work, their prestige continues to be very high.
Villagers raise their hands in the traditional gesture of respect when they meet an official and address him with the respectful pronoun "t'an."
Women still squat or kneel to talk to him.

Prestige is not only a reason for wanting to
belong to the civil service. It also motivates
people to seek advancement. Great respect is paid
to rank in Thai society, and any villager can tell
the difference between a high ranking official and
a clerk. Moreover, a high official enjoys not only
the respect of the citizenry but also that of his
subordinates in the civil service. The respect of
official subordinates is probably more rewarding
than the respect of citizens. For, other officials
constitute a civil servant's reference group.
Their respect and deference are important in defin-
ing his self concept, and the status hierarchy most
salient to him is that of the civil service.

The civil service also offers the opportunity
to be of public service and most of the officials
at Central District mentioned this as a source of
satisfaction. It is difficult to assess the importance of the motive to serve because service is a
part of the official ideology, but it is no doubt
true that most people find it pleasant to be of
service to others, if only because it brings gratitude and permits one to take a flattering view of
himself. The opportunity to be of service that a
civil service career offers was not included in the
list of rewards in the final form of the survey
questionnaire. However, in the pretest form it was

listed, and all of the respondents in the pretest chose service as the most important reward of a civil service career.

Finally, the civil service offers the opportunity to add to one's income in various more or less illegal ways. Bribery and corruption are problems in every society, but one must understand that in Thailand it is not always easy to tell just where the borderline between official honesty and dishonesty lies. A particular act may appear dishonest or not depending on the circumstances. For example, an official who requires citizens to pay fees in order to get him to carry out his duties is clearly corrupt, but this occurs very rarely. Most often, a citizen will make an official a present of money or some other gift, and the official will expedite the citizen's business for him. No word connecting these two acts will be spoken. For example, a citizen of Central District who applies for a permit to own a gun must wait several weeks or even months to get it, but if he gives appropriate gifts to certain officials, he will find that the procedure takes much less time. This may be bribery, but the officials can say in all honesty that they have not demanded money from the citizen.

An even more ambiguous example was recounted by one of the deputy district officers of Central District. It seems that when he bought his motorcycle, the shop owner sold it to him for a very low price. Now, this shopkeeper must go to the district to pay taxes and to renew his permit to keep a shop, and the deputy district officer is a position to expedite this business for him. Was the motorcycle a bribe?

The question of whether an act is corrupt or not is often a matter of the nature of the rules rather than of the act (Scott, 1972a:7). For example, it is not uncommon for Central District to collect money from local citizens for projects of public benefit, and probably some part of this money is used by officials for personal expenses. However, any private charitable organization takes a part of the money it collects to pay the salaries of its permanent staff; so the difference clearly lies in the rules and not in the acts.

The point is that whenever an official has rules to enforce or services to perform, he can receive gratitude for not enforcing the rules or for performing the services (Blau, 1963:215). If he prefers, he can arrange to receive cash or other tangibles instead of gratitude. In the next chapter we shall see that Thai officials often bend the rules and perform services for people and that cash income is not always the reason for doing it. Nevertheless, various forms of "corruption" are important sources of income for some officials.

Conclusions

We have seen that Thai officials are motivated to seek advancement by the inadequacy of salaries at lower levels. In addition, they work for security, for autonomy in their work, for prestige for the public good and for informally earned income. It has been shown that the achievement of these goals is only partly contingent on doing good work. The cumbersome and unstandardized system of evaluation and the high centralization of the power to reward officials render it nearly impossible to reward them fairly. Only those who bring themselves dramatically to the notice of their superiors at several levels and who build good personal relations with them can expect to be rewarded regularly.

Thus, in constructing his role the district official must balance the demands that are made on him to do certain kinds of work with the requirement of bringing himself to his superior's notice. Moreover, he must accomplish the latter in a way that makes him appear trustworthy. He must impress the superiors with his dedication to his work and with his loyalty to them, and this must be accomplished in a setting in which power is divided among several superiors at different levels. In order to do all this he must receive assistance through social exchange as will be shown in the next chapter.

NOTES

1.   The system of grades described here is gradually being eliminated in favor of a more detailed system of position classification. It is not yet clear what difference, if any, this will make in the behavior of officials. In any case the system of grades was still in use at the time of this research.

2.   Thai education below the university level includes seven years of primary school knows as Prat'om Suksa one through seven, three years of secondary school, called Mat'ayom Suksa one through three, and two years of university preparatory

67

school called Mat'ayom Sɯksa four and five. In addition there are a number of technical training schools which offer certificates below the baccalaureate. These include the Forestry School at Nan, the Agricultural School at Chiengmai, schools for training public health workers, and teacher training colleges. Graduates of all schools from Mat'a yom Sɯksa three to just below the baccalaureate. enter the civil service at the fourth grade.

3. These examinations generally have little relevance to the work an official does or might do. They cannot be very relevant because they are examinations for grade promotions and therefore do not test competence in the work of particular positions.

4. Officially, the report is written by the official's immediate superior, but in practice each official writes his own report which is then signed by his superior.

5. This is true in practice but not in theory. All communication from the district to the province must be from the district officer to the governor. The former should never communicate directly with the provincial section heads. In practice, however, the district officer's recommendations merely pass through the hands of a clerk who puts the governor's stamp on them and passes them on to the appropriate sections. The governor does not really see the recommendations until after they have been reviewed by the sections.

6. In calculating these percentages, two sections were eliminated from the totals. The Local Administration Section was eliminated because its members received raises in excess of the 6 percent quota due to the fact that several special raises were given to officials who worked in "sensitive" districts along the border with Laos. The village Schools Section was eliminated because its members come under the Provincial Administrative Organization which means that the final authority to grant raises to these officials lies at the province.

5. Work and Social Exchange in a District Office

We now turn out attention from the structural situation in which Thai district officials act to the patterns of their interaction. In this chapter, we shall see how district officials deal with the problems they face and how the structural factors that have been reviewed channel their behavior into predictable and regular forms. In doing his work an official tries to earn the trust of his superior and colleagues in order to increase his chances of advancement and in order to obtain increased autonomy in his work. The trust of superiors is earned by doing good work and by building good personal relations with them. Each of these includes several different sorts of activities which are discussed in the following section. The process of building the trust of colleagues will be discussed later in this chapter.

DOING GOOD WORK

An official who wants to earn the trust of his superiors and to advance in the civil service must ordinarily do good work. Siffin (1966:153) speaks of productivity as occupying "an obscure and secondary place" among the values of the Thai civil service, and other writers who worked in Thailand during the 1950's appear to agree with him (Riggs, 1966:327; Shor, 1962; Horrigan, 1959:203). On the other hand, the findings of Neher (1969:139-40) and Suwannabul (1971:90), who did their work a decade later, support the view that good work is necessary for advancement, or at least that the officials whom they studied firmly believed that to be the case. The findings of this study support the conclusions of the latter group. The officials of Central District unquestionably said that good work was important for

69

advancement and acted as if they believed it to be true.

The reason for the increase in the importance of productivity appears to be that in the nineteen sixties the threat of communist subversion and ethnic separatism in some regions led the rulers of Thailand to feel a need to improve their relations with the citizens and to raise their levels of living. Consequently, broad programs of rural development and public relations were undertaken (Scoville and Dalton, 1974; Roth, 1976). These programs have been quite successful in some ways. The number of miles of roads has been vastly increased, many new schools have been built, and many wells have been dug. (See Ingram, 1971, for data on Thai economic growth.) To accomplish these things pressure was placed on officials to improve their productivity (defined as the completion of projects, not as success in development in any larger sense).

The extent and nature of the change may be gauged by comparing Horrigan's (1959) findings on district officials' perceptions of the routes to advancement with the findings of Neher (1969). Horrigan's respondents listed as routes to advancement flattery, presents to superiors, and procuring for superiors. Technical qualifications were listed only in fourth place, and output was not listed at all. In contrast, a district officer interviewed by Neher (1969:139) said:

> If I am to fulfill my ambition (to be a governor), I must stand out as the best district officer. I have therefore established a master plan for Sung (his district), the only long-range plan for any district officer in Chiang Mai province. I have invited the governor and provincial officials to visit my district so that they can see for themselves the progress that we are making.

More general support for the notion that productivity has become important to district officials comes from my own research. Of the district officials surveyed, 57 percent said that they worked overtime at least once a week, and an additional 23 percent did so at least twice a month. Moreover, 96 percent of the officials said that they had spent their own money to assure the success of their work, even though they could not hope to be reimbursed.

70

These findings attest to the importance attributed
by officials to productivity. However, in interpreting this the reader must remember Blau's
(1963:56) finding that the procedure used to evalu-
ate a worker's performance will influence strongly
the nature of that performance: the worker will
put his effort into doing the things that make him
look good when he is evaluated.

One of the structural characteristics of the
Thai civil service is that the formal method of
evaluation is cumbersome and understandardized.
Another characteristic is that the decision to reward good work is always made by someone who is
distant from it both hierarchically and geographic-
ally. This means that work which shows dramatic
results that are easily seen from a distance is
likely to take on special significance. Officials
who want to advance in their careers must concentrate their efforts on doing the things that draw
the favorable attention of superiors and avoids
spending time on things that do not have this effect.

Construction and Other Dramatic Projects[1]

One sort of accomplishment that brings favorable attention is a construction project. A road,
an irrigation canal, a school, or a water system
that an official has built can be made to appear impressive in an annual report. So, district officials put a good deal of time and effort into construction, and they report construction work in
great detail. The importance of construction leads
to the relative neglect of equally important but
less dramatic sorts of work. For example, public
health education is an important part of the public
health officer's job and one which might bring significant improvements in the health of the villagers.
But, the public health officer does very little
health education, and he does not stress the educational function of his subordinates in the commune
health stations. The public health officer's main
effort is directed toward the building of rural
water supply systems.

The one exception to this lack of interest in
public health education is significant because it
supports my contention that what makes educational
work unattractive is its lack of dramatic results.
Great stress is laid by the public health officer
on persuading villagers to build sanitary privies.
For this purpose both technical and financial

assistance are made available to the peasants. If
we ask why so much stress is laid on this particular program, the answer is of course that its educational efforts lead to construction projects
which can be enumerated and described in reports.

A project does not have to involve construction in order to be dramatic. An imaginative official may be able to design other sorts of attention getting work. For example, the district
officer of Central District had a "village visit"
program that brought him favorably to the attention
of Northern Province's governor. The program was
a response to the government's policy of building
the good will of the villagers in order to fight
communism. Two village visits were organized each
month: every other weekend the regular services of
the district office were provided in a distant
village. A weekend's activities began on Friday
night when the deputy district officers would arrive
in a village and show a movie. Villagers would
come from miles around to see it, and the officials
would announce the following day's program.

On Saturday morning the heads of several of
the district's sections would arrive to provide
services. The public health officer would give in-
oculations; the registration section would perform
marriages, issue identity cards, enter people in
the household register and so on; land title deeds
that had been applied for would be passed out by
the Land Section; the Agricultural Extension Section would give advice to farmers about crops,
fertilizers, and insecticides. On ordinary days
the villagers had to go to the district office for
these services at some expense to themselves, but
on this day the services were provided in their own
village. The village visits were successful, and
they became a large feather in the district officer's cap. He invited the governor to attend
one, and after seeing it the governor ordered the
other district officers of the province to organize
village visits after the pattern of Central District's.

Dramatic projects like these bring an official
to his superiors' notice in a big way, but they are
costly. For the village visits, the district officer had to get fuel for the district's vehicles
(the district s fuel allowance was not nearly
enough); he had to get a sound system and a gene-
rator in each village; he had to obtain a free
movie every other weekend; he had to have signs

made to designate the places where the various sections were set up; finally he had to feed all of the officials who took part in the village visits. He had to do these things in spite of the fact that the district's budget did not provide resources for any of them.

Raising Resources Locally [2]

In order to obtain resources for such dramatic projects funds are raised in the local community by district officials. Moreover, even when it might be possible to obtain the funds for a project from the Central Administration, officials sometimes prefer to use local resources. For, the statement that a project costing many thousands of baht was carried out largely without the use of government funds looks especially good on a report. The result is that although regulations prohibit officials from asking citizens for resources, fund raising is one of the most important aspects of their roles as is shown by the survey responses. Of the district officials surveyed, 65 percent had asked for resources from merchants or other citizens.

Resources are raised locally in various ways. One of the most common ways is through donations from the merchants in Northtown. Since Northtown produces a very large proportion of the wealth of Northern Province, this is an easy way for the officials of Central District to raise money. For example, the merchants of the town gave about $1500 in cash and in kind to finance the training camp for the district's athletic team, and at T'ǫd Kat'in, an occasion on which Thai people traditionally make donations to help their local temples, the district officials raised a substantial sum to rebuild a temple primary school in a remote village.

In addition to large donations for special projects, the merchants of Northtown are frequently asked for small donations in kind. For example, when the village visit program required some signs, the district officials got a local weaving mill to donate cloth and asked a movie house owner to have his sign painter make the signs. The district also has a continual shortage of vehicles, and businessmen are sometimes asked for the loan of theirs.

In outlying districts which lack large market towns, fewer resources can be raised, and consequently much less can be done. When resources are raised, they must be obtained indirectly from villagers instead of directly from merchants. For example, the district officer of one district persuaded a man who shows motion pictures at temple fairs to donate to the district the proceeds from some special showings in order to support the district's athletic team.

Fewer resources can be raised from villagers than from merchants because most villagers are poor, but one thing they can provide is voluntary labor for projects like roads, bridges, or canals. As pointed out in an earlier chapter, the villagers understand the benefits of development and are anxious to obtain them. In addition, work on a project of this sort is seen as a way of helping a government official who might later be in a position to do one a favor. Thus, social exchange between officials and villagers emerges.

This social exchange is in fact a two step process. The district officials deal directly with village headmen and other wealthy villagers, those identified by Neher (1972) as "politicals," and these in turn deal with the rest of the villagers. That is, a development official anxious to build a road or a water supply system will enlist the support of the village headman and other influential villagers. These in turn will mobilize the labor of the mass the villagers. This "clientelist" (Powell, 1970; Scott, 1972) chain has become a key point in the political integration of the Thai state as will be discussed in more detail later.

It has been mentioned that in general it is illegal for officials to ask for donations from citizens (except for labor). Resource procurement also leads officials into activities which are illegal in other ways. For example, in order to build a certain bridge, lumber had to be obtained. The amount required was too large to be obtained as a donation, and no money was available to buy it. So, trees were cut in the forest illegally. (Limits on cutting are imposed in order to conserve the trees.) This was possible because the forests officer who was supposed to enforce the regulation and who is also a subordinate of the district officer recognized the importance of the bridge to the district.

Officials are not limited in the search for resources to those that can be obtained from private citizens. Resources are also obtained from other state agencies, and 61 percent of the district

74

officials responding to the survey had obtained
resources from other agencies. For example, the
Accelerated Rural Development Program (ARD) has a
good supply of construction machinery, and when
Central District officials need a tractor or a road
grader they often borrowed one from ARD.

A really enterprising official may also obtain resources from friends in his department in
Bangkok. For, while the district's budget is never
large enough, it can be increased by skillful entre-
preneurship. For example, a headmaster in a district I visited needed some money to improve his
school. So, he invested in a trip to Bangkok and
took a highly placed friend out to lunch. Thus, he
obtained the funds he needed.

Returns to Those Who Provide Resources: Social Exchange in Action

The reader may already suspect that the people
who donate resources to the district do not do so
solely out of a patriotic desire to contribute to
the development of their country or of their community. This is not to say that altruistic motives
are absent. Giving to "good causes" is recognized
everywhere as a desirable thing to do, and therefore someone who gives is entitled to take a morally
flattering view of himself. The reward value of a
positive self concept undoubtedly serves to motivate some altruistic behavior. Moreover, an act of
public generosity may be recognized and the giver
accorded gratitude and honor by the community.

In addition, Thai Buddhism teaches that there
is a Law of Karma according to which a good act inevitably brings a good return to the actor, and a
bad act brings a bad return. Although it is not
always apparent in this life that the Law of Karma
is fulfilled, one can expect it to be fulfilled in
future incarnations, or, as some educated Thais now
assert, in the lives of the children of the actor.
Of the meritorious acts which bring good returns,
one that is specifically mentioned in Buddhist
teachings as they are taught to Thai children in
school is the act of helping to carry out projects
of community value (Krom Wichakan, 1970:83).

The Law of Karma is not an empty formula to
most Thai people. An official of Northern Province
said,

I help freely and as much as I can. And

75

I never help just a little bit, either. I
don't ask for any return for the work I do
except for the merit which I am accumulating.
I do good, and good will return to me one
day. I don't ask for a return today, tomor-
row, or the next, but in the future or after
I have died the good that I have done will
help me to receive good and not to have to
fall into sufferings and hardship. This even
reaches to my descendants, my children. When
I have died, people will see the good that I
have done, and so my children's lives will be
made easier. That is what I hope for.

However, not everyone is sufficiently motivated
by the desire for personal satisfaction, gratitude,
honor, or merit to give generously to the district's
projects. Some people ask for more concrete and
immediate rewards, and even those who are altruis-
tically motivated help more readily if there is some
immediate return to them as well. How do officials
of the district reward those who help?

One reward that an official can give to a
citizen is expressed in the Thai phrase "amnuaj
k'wamsaduag." This means several things. First,
it means to expedite someone's business. A Thai
businessman or farmer must often go to the district
office to obtain or renew a permit, to register a
vehicle or a draft animal, or to pay taxes. This
can be very time consuming, but a person who has
been helpful to the district's officials will find
it much less so. Likewise, a village headman must
often go to the district office on business for the
people of his village, and he will find that if they
have cooperated well with the district's work, his
own work may be accomplished without undue delay.

"Amnuaj k'wamsaduag" also means to avoid placing a procedural obstacle in someone's way. For
example, a person who wants to own a gun in Thailand must be certified to be of good moral character. This requires a police investigation, and
the police are very busy. So, it may take several
months, but a person who has been generous to the
district will find that the investigation can be
completed in a few days. Survey results support
notion that the practice of amnuaj k'wamsaduag is
quite common in Thailand; 97 percent of the district
officials said that they had engaged in the practice.

Sometimes, amnuaj k'wamsaduag involves bending

the regulations a little. Once, when I was in an outlying commune with a deputy district officer, we spent the night at the home of the kamnan, and a woman came to see him with a registration problem. It seemed that her son was of the age when he had to register for military conscription, but he could not do so because his name was not in the household register and could not be entered into it because at the time of his birth his mother had not recorded it officially. The proper procedure in such a case would have been to call witnesses and make an official investigation to establish the identity of the young man, but that would have been cumbersome and, since the kamnan knew the woman and her son, unnessary. Fortunately, the kamnan had some old birth certificates of the type that had been used when the young man was born, and with the deputy district officer's agreement he issued a birth certificate (dated 20 years earlier) for the young man and told the mother to go and get her son's name placed in the household register. This sort of thing is quite common in Thailand as is shown by the fact that 43 percent of the district officials surveyed said that they would break minor rules to help people if they thought that the infractions would not be detected and would cause no harm.

This example illustrates well the operation of the two-step clientelist chain of social exchange between villagers and officials. The woman went for a favor, not to an official, but to her kamnan. The help he was able to give her indebted her to him and so increased his power in the commune. It probably had an effect on other villagers, too, by demonstrating that he could and would help them. As a result he would find it easier to mobilize the villagers for district development projects, and if he was successful in doing so, he would indebt the officials to him and so increase his ability to obtain favors for himself or his villagers.

The above example also illustrates the role or trust in social exchange. Neither the kamnan nor the official were concerned merely to reward others who had been helpful. Instead, they sought opportunities to assist citizens in special ways in order to build their trust. One never knows when one may need to call on others for help, and therefore one should take advantage of opportunities to earn their gratitude and to instill in them the belief that one can be trusted to help when they need

77

it. By the same token, when an ordinary villager has an opportunity to help a potential patron, he is inclined to do so in order to show that he is a person who deserves consideration. The process of social exchange is one in which favors can be asked, not ordinarily a process of bargaining or of negotiation.

The district can also amnuaj k'wamsaduag for other official agencies that are helpful. For example, the Accelerated Rural Development Program (ARD) must have the cooperation of the villagers in order to accomplish its goals. Access to the villagers is monopolized by the district officer through his control of the village headmen. So, he can be of great help to ARD, and thus make some return for ARD's loans of its construction equipment.

The social exchange of resources for amnuaj k'wamsaduag is nicely summed up in the words of one of the deputy district officers of Central District:

> Suppose the district needs a vehicle, as was the situation at T'ǫd Kat'in I was able to get a bus and a band of musicians and other things as well. When it comes to asking for money, I can't do that because in my work I don't deal much with people who have money, but I can get the villagers to help in other ways. . . .
>
> But there is one thing you should know: our people are likely to be most helpful to whoever they think has the most power because they hope to receive favors in return. Suppose a villager comes to the office to get permission to have a gun; he comes to see me because he knows me, and he asks for help. If I can't help him he will not be interested in helping me after that. So, anyone who wants to be successful at development work must first be good at getting things done at the district office.
>
> So, he comes to the office, and I go to (a registration official), and I say that this fellow has been very helpful with the work of development; he is OK; help him a little. (The registration official) says, "All right; here, write the application." Then I go to the district officer, and I tell him that this man has been very helpful; he has asked for a gun, it is not against any regulation. Help him a little. So, the district officer helps

(by approving the application immediately).
Now, when I can do that sort of thing
the villagers see right away that it is worth
their while to work with me. They go and
say to their friends. "(The respondent) is
mot just good out here in the villages. He
can do things for you at the district office,
too." If I were to concern myself only with
the field work at the office, there would be
no way for me to accomplish anything.[3]

Amnuaj k'wamsaduag is not the only thing that
the district officials have to offer to citizens
who help them. Permitting tax evasion is also used
as a reward. Income taxes and business taxes are
paid at the district's Revenue Section. Each
business estimates his business volume, and his
estimate is used as the basis for calculating how
much business tax (a turnover tax on business volume) he owes. If the district revenue officer believes that a businessman has underestimated his
business volume, he may report the case to the provincial revenue section which may the investigate
it. Now, it is well known in Thailand that businessmen generally underestimate their business
volume for tax purposes, or as Lewchalermwong
(1972:81) puts it, "In Thailand, tax evasion is
not an unusual phenomenon and does not provide
strong public condemnation against tax evaders. .
. ." A very considerable proportion of the tax is
evaded: the Revenue Officer of one district esti-
mated to me that most businessmen underestimate
their business volume by approximately 70 percent.
Naturally, in this situation businessmen are
anxious to have the good will of the district officer. They are glad to purchase it for a few thou-
sand baht in aid to the district's work rather than
risk having to pay several times the amount in
taxes if they are investigated. In effect, then,
the district officials subject the local businessmen to a genial form of blackmail: help us or pay
higher taxes is the implied threat, although naturally nothing of the sort is ever said.
Permitting tax evasion is not the only way
that a district official can help a local businessman to make money. Certain sections are, themselves, large purchasers of some goods like construction materials. The district officer can also
influence the selection of the entertainment con-
cessionnaires for the big fair that is held in the

province's most important temple each year. On one occasion, a man who shows movies at temple fairs all over the region agreed to do a showing at one of the district's village visits. At the same time, he expressed an interest in obtaining the motion picture concession for the next year's fair, and the district officer agreed to see what he could do.

Elite villagers may benefit from this sort of patronage as well as town businessmen. For example, after a road was completed to one village, the headman received a license to operate a bus service on the road. In other cases, wealthy villagers may become distributers of gasoline and diesel fuel. Thus, at each level the participants in the system benefit from its operation.

Political Implications of Local Fund Raising

Let us stop for a moment and consider the political causes and implications of the practice of raising resources locally by district officials. Why must district officials raise resources locally? The reason is, of course, that the budgetary allocations they receive from the central government are insufficient for their needs. But why, we must ask, are the budgetary allocations insufficient? Part of the answer is that Thailand is a poor country with many pressing needs, and resources are by definition never sufficient to meet all needs.

That is not the whole answer, however. Another part is that the state lacks funds to do more because it does not collect taxes effectively. The widespread practice of tax evasion already alluded to leads into a vicious circle: the district must raise resources locally because the state cannot give it more money, and the state cannot give it more money because the districts do not collect taxes effectively. The districts do not collect taxes effectively because they need to motivate businessmen to give generously to help the district's development efforts. The system is self systaining.

Moreover, it has significant political consequences. Chapter One described briefly the alliance between the army and the business community which is the base of power of the government of Thailand. Here, we find the same alliance repeated at the local level except that here it is not the army but the district officials who are allied to business community and the village elite. Just as the national business elite provided resources for the officials of the central government in return for favors, so the local businessmen and elite provide resources for the officials of the district. At the national level this alliance effectively tied the interests of the official elite to those of business, and a new bureaucratic-capitalist elite was formed. Now a similar cycle of events appears to have occurred in the countryside. Economic development has created a business and agricultural elite that controls the resources needed for further development. In order to obtain these resources, district officials have entered into the alliance with the local elites found by this research, but the rural masses have thereby been excluded from participation in policy making.

The political alliance between local elites and officials also reacts back on economic development, influencing its direction by distorting the officials' view of their district's rural development needs. District officials pride themselves on being in close contact with the villagers and knowing their desires. In fact, however, contacts between district officials and villagers are mediated by the elite villagers who serve as headmen and kamnans, as my findings and those of other researchers (Neher, 1972; Moerman, 1969) show. Therefore, district officials know the desires of villagers almost exclusively as they are transmitted by elite village leaders, and consequently the policy bias in favor of forms of development that benefit those leaders is further reinforced.

For instance, the development of cooperative credit societies has long been hamstrung for lack of funds in spite of the growing indebtedness and tenancy in the countryside. Naturally, the local economic elites, many of whom are small money lenders, are reluctant to donate resources for cooperatives -- so they languish. In the same way, although roads are built to improve the marketing of crops, nothing is done to provide grain storage facilities that might permit a peasant to market his crop when the price is high rather than at harvest time. Under these conditions, poor peasants are at the mercy of the market, and many lose their land through inability to repay mortgage loans (Roth, 1976:1060). Thus, while rural economic expansion proceeds, it does so in a way that leads to increasing inequality in the countryside.

Avoiding Conspicuous Failure

An ambitious official must not only produce dramatic accomplishments in his work to draw the attention of his superiors, he must also avoid drawing their attention by conspicuous failures. One way an official may do this is to use his own money to insure the success of a project if he cannot obtain the resources for it elsewhere. For example, a deputy district officer at Central District was building a road, and the tractor he was using got stuck in the sand. In order to pull it out a heavy truck was needed. The district had no such truck, but he got one from a local army base. However, while the district's budget paid for the fuel for the truck, no per diem was available for the drivers and other men who came to help. So, the deputy district officer had to treat them to meals for two days at a cost of more than 200 baht. This officer was a third grade official with a salary of less than 1500 baht per month, which means that he contributed a sizeable part of his month's salary to the success of this project alone.

Officials use their own money to avoid failure in office work as well as in field work. During the year of this research national elections were to be held, and Central District's officials were ordered to prepare voter registration lists. This took a great deal of time and, more important, quite a lot of paper which was in short supply because of recent increases in its price. The official in charge of the preparation of the lists was unable to get enough paper from the provincial supply center, but he did not feel that the lack of supplies would be accepted as an explanation of his failure to get his work done on time: a good official can get the supplies he needs. So, he spent his own money for a ream of paper and at the same time renewed his struggle with the province. He finally got some more paper, but he was never reimbursed for the paper he had bought. The survey results indicate that the use by officials of their own money to assure the success of their work is widespread in Thailand: 96 percent of the respondents had done so.

Another sort of failure that Central District's officials try to avoid is the failure to turn in reports which district officials must send annually to their provincial and departmental superiors. If a report is late or improperly prepared, the district officer will be criticized by the governor, and that will make the district official who pre-pared the report look bad. So, officials try very hard to get their work done on time and in the proper form even if they must work overtime to do so. I often observed officials doing paperwork at home in the evening or on weekends at Central District, and of the survey respondents, 57 percent had worked overtime at least once a week and an additional 23 percent at least twice a month.

The effort to get reports in on time and in the proper form does not always extend to assuring that their content is entirely accurate. Statistical reports in Thailand are notoriously unreliable, and district officials often estimate numbers while sitting at their desks rather than spend the time to go into the field and count things. The large number of reports submitted and the heavy work loads of high officials assure that the accuracy of statistics will rarely be checked. So, spending time on research would bring little reward and would take time from more rewarding activities.

In addition to the obvious kinds of overtime work that officials do, an ambitious person may visit his superior at home in order to have opportunities to run errands or to take care of emergencies for the superior. The reason for this practice should be clear: it brings the official to the superior's notice quite forcibly. Just as dramatic projects with easily understood results look good on annual reports, so working directly for a superior after official hours causes the superior to see the official as ambitious, hardworking, and loyal. Of the respondents to the survey, 97 percent said that it was important for officials to be prepared to receive and follow the orders of superiors outside of official hours.

In sum, doing good work is important to a Thai official, but the structural constraints under which he acts channel his behavior into directions which the phrase "doing good work" might not at first appear to imply. The cumbersome system of evaluation when combined with the centralization of authority causes officials to place a disproportionate emphasis on large, dramatic projects at the expense of other, equally important kinds of work. Such large projects are very expensive, and budgetary funds are not available for them because at both the local level and the national level power is held by a coalition of officials and businessmen who permit widespread tax evasion. However,

while it may be impossible to collect taxes effectively, individual tax evaders are vulnerable to
pressure and therefore can be persuaded to give resources for the district's work.[4] In addition to
condoning tax evasion, district officials also are
able to amnuaj k'wamsaduag for ditizens, and that
gives the latter an incentive to help the officials
when they can.

We have seen that district officials go out of
their way to build the trust of merchants and of
elite villagers in order to be able to demand favors
from them at a later time, and the citizens do the
same to the officials. Thus, a process of social
exchange emerges which is oriented not toward bargaining over specific items to be changed but toward
the building and maintaining of relationships which
are perceived as dependable sources of rewards.

In addition to carrying out dramatic projects
to draw the favorable attention of superiors, officials also try hard to avoid conspicuous failures.
They use substantial amounts of their own money to
prevent the failure of their projects, and they work
overtime quite often in order to get reports in on
time and in the proper form. However, the overload
of paperwork at higher levels which is caused by the
centralization of power in the hands of certain
officials, together with the lack of staff to assist
those officials, renders it impossible for the officials who read the reports to check their accuracy.
Consequently, relatively little effort is expended
by district officials to insure the accuracy of the
reports they submit.

BUILDING GOOD PERSONAL RELATIONS WITH SUPERIORS

Performing Personal Service And Going In The Back
Of The House

A Thai official who wants to earn the trust of
his superiors must be prepared not only to do good
work but also to serve them in unofficial ways. In
this, Thai officials are quite different from American officials, of whom Blau (1963:177) has said,

. . . associations between particular individuals are valued . . . but the fact that
mutual obligations are definitely circum-
scribed, in contradistinction to those in
friendships, precludes unexpected personal
service that would disrupt bureaucratic activities.

84

The range of personal services that Thai officials can expect from one another is much wider than it is among American officials, and Thai superiors, especially, are inclined to use their subordinates for various personal services that would be regarded as improper in the American context. Most district officials expect to have to perform such services, as is shown by the fact that 69 percent of the district officials responding to the survey said that it was important for an official to be ready to serve his superior in ways outside of his official duties. The extra work that Thai officials perform includes a variety of sorts of official and personal duties.

Within official contexts, officials are often asked to help with the work of other sections or with special jobs. For example, when the deputy director of the Department of Local Administration visited Central District, the officials of all the sections were asked to assist in organizing the reception, even though most of them have no official connection with that department. However, it was in the interest of the district officer to show up well before his superior, and he required the help of all of his subordinates in the effort to do so.

Official work shades off into personal service in the receptions that are organized for visiting dignitaries. When the district officer gives a luncheon for an official of his department, the deputy district officers will be asked to make the arrangements, and the clerks will be asked to wait at table. It is difficult to tell whether these are official duties of these persons or not. In principle, they are not official duties, but such receptions are so much an accepted part of official life that most Thai people would probably say that arranging them is a part of the job.

From such quasi-personal services, we move to strictly personal services. An official may be asked to pick up his superior's children at school or to run an errand for his wife. Officials vary a good deal in their attitudes toward performing such services for the families of their superiors. All officials will do them if asked, but only a minority will seek out opportunities to do so. Most officials seem to regard such activities as what we would call "bootlicking" and prefer to avoid them when they can.

However, most officials feel that they must visit their superiors at home from time to time, especially on occasions like New Year's Day or the superiors' birthdays. Virtually everyone goes to visit his immediate superior on these occasions to pay respect to him, and an official who is ambitious may also visit the homes of superiors further up the line. For example, 75 percent of the district officials in the survey said that they visited the homes of the governors of their provinces on their birthdays and on New Year's Day.

Some officials make a practice of visiting superiors' homes at other times as well. This is done partly in order to have opportunities to receive orders from the superiors as I have described, but it may also have the purpose of getting to know their families and of taking opportunities to be of service to their households. This practice is known as "going in the back of the house," and it is widely regarded as an effective method of obtaining advancement. However, most officials regard going in the back of the house as an unsatisfactory road to advancement. While all officials visit their superiors from time to time, it appears that relatively few deliberately try to build careers through relations with the families of high officials. As one man put it,

> If you go in the back of the house without having done any work, you will do well, but . . . it won't give a feeling of pride, ... you do well because your superior has raised you up without your having any ability.

In addition to being distasteful to some officials, there are some who do not go in the back of the house because it is costly in time. Several of Central District's officials and more than a third of the survey respondents held other jobs or farmed in addition to their official work, and the time taken up by these unofficial jobs precluded going in the back of the house.

An official going in the back of the house may also bring his superiors small presents from time to time. These presents are not bribes in any sense. Their value is much too small. An official might bring a small bag of fruit or some sweets purchased in the market. Such presents fall into the category of symbolic gestures designed to assure a superior of the loyalty of a subordinate.

Table 5.1

Importance of Building Personal Relations with Superiors

How important are such things as joining in a superior's merit making ceremonies, visiting him on his birthday and New Year's Day to wish him good luck or bringing him small presents. . .?

	Not Important	Not Very Important	Important	Very Important	
In order to get work done	3% (2)	27% (21)	62% (48)	9% (7)	100%* (78)
In order to obtain advancement	6% (5)	33% (26)	33% (26)	27% (21)	100% (78)

*Figures do not total to 100% because of rounding

Table 5.1 shows that a substantial proportion of district officials feel that building personal relations with superiors is an important thing to do. The table shows that making various sorts of symbolic gestures helps to obtain advancement in two ways. It helps directly because it leads to good personal relations with superiors, but it also helps indirectly by making it easier to get one's work done. The reader will recall that a superior can delay his subordinate's work by not approving it quickly if the subordinate is not trusted. A superior's trust may be increased by symbolic gestures that express loyalty, and so they help to speed up one's work. Moreover, good personal relations with superiors may be exploited to obtain extra budgetary funds and so make possible larger accomplishments. In short, building a superior's trust through symbolic gestures is not only a substitute for good work, it may also be a part of doing it.

The importance of building relations with superiors is the basis of the advantage in obtaining double raises enjoyed by officials stationed in the provincial capital. The officials of the provincial capital can make themselves available for special work assignments at the homes of their provincial superiors or visit them with small presents more

easily than the officials from distant districts
can. The latter must often travel long distances
and even stay overnight in the provincial capital
in order to visit their superiors.

A really ambitious and successful official must
contrive to build good relations with his superiors
in his department in Bangkok as well. This cannot
be done entirely from the provinces because a provincial official does not have sufficiently frequent occasions to visit Bangkok. In order to
build good relations with his superiors in the
central administration of this department, an official must spend some time working there. So, we
can observe that in the careers of successful district and provincial officials, periods of work in
rural areas alternate with periods spent in the
central, departmental offices. During the time
that he is in Bangkok, an official will get to know
people in his department. Then, when he is out in
the provinces, he will try to do notably good work
which will come to the attention of his friends,
and he will try to keep the friendships alive by
periodic visits to the department. He will bring
his friends some fruit or perhaps a regional deli-
cacy from the province where he is stationed. They
in turn will take him out drinking, and so the
friendship will be maintained. Of the district
officials responding to the survey, three fourths
said that they visited friends in their departments
whenever they went to Bangkok.

Showing Proper Respect

One aspect of building relations with superiors
that deserves mention because of its importance in
Thai society is the display of proper respect. A
Thai official must always display respect for his
superiors. A section head may bow when he enters
the district officer's office. He will probably
"wai" in the traditional gesture of respect with
the hands together in fron of the chest when he
meets the district officer, and he will almost certainly speak to him using the respectful pronoun
"t'an." Of the district officials surveyed, 92
percent said that they addressed their district
officers either as "t'an" or as "t'an nai amp'oe."
("Nai amp'oe" means a district officer.)
The role of such expressions of respect in interaction is somewhat different in Thailand from
what it is in the United States. American society
is quite egalitarian in ideology, and elaborate

respect is not regularly paid to superiors. So, an
American who is prepared to use respectful forms can
"butter up" his superior in this way. If he says,
"Yes, sir," and "No sir," and stands when his superior enters the room he can earn points, so to
speak, at least if he does not go so far that it
becomes obvious what he is trying to accomplish
(Jones, 1964).

Thai society is much more hierarchical in its
ideology. Respect paid to superiors is the norm,
and anyone who failed to show respect would give
serious offense. Therefore, the person who pays
respect to his superior does not gain much thereby
except that he shows that he has been properly
brought up and that he knows the obligations of his
position. On the other hand, the person who failed
to show respect would lose a great deal.

The need to pay proper respect leads to a great
deal of ceremonial behavior. For example, at a
village meeting which was attended by several officials, the village headman and the kamnan, everyone
waited for the district officer to appear. When he
arrived, all the officials, the headman and the
kamnan lined up beside his jeep to receive him as he
stepped out. They all "wai-ed" and he "wai-ed" in
return. This sort of ceremonial is a regular feature of Thai official life.

The demands of respect and deference can become quite onerous when a very high superior is involved. For this reason, an official who has no
special business with a superior and no special
reason to want to be seen by him will leave the
scene rather than meet the superior. When the
governor of Northern Province visited Central District's offices, a number of officials fled to a
back room where they would not have to meet him.
For, while nothing was to be gained by meeting him,
a great deal could be lost by being seen to fail in
respect.

Showing respect also includes providing entertainment for visiting dignitaries. When a high
ranking official from Bangkok visits Northern Province, the officials from his department in the
province spend a good deal of time preparing for
his arrival and considerable amounts of their own
money for his entertainment. When the Deputy Director General of the Department of Local Administration was to come to Central District to open a regional training session, one could see quite clearly
the importance which the district officer gave to

the preparations for his reception in the amounts of time which he and his subordinates gave to the job. The senior deputy district officer gave several days to the work in spite of the fact that this meant that his regular work was delayed. The district officer, himself gave several hours to the job of supervising the preparation of the meeting hall. When the deputy director general came, all the district officers of the province were on hand, although they had nothing particular to do there, and they had to leave their regular work to attend.

That evening the governor hosted a party for the visitor which was attended by all of the high ranking officials of the Department of Local Administration in the province. The next day a party was hosed by the deputy governor (palad ɓangwat) at lunch, and again it was well attended. These parties were held in restaurants and were paid for out of the pockets of the officials who hosted them. When the reader remembers how low Thai official salaries are, he will begin to see the importance of such ceremonials.

The necessity of entertaining visiting dignitaries is a problem for all provincial officials and a problem for the civil service as a whole because it provides an incentive for corruption. An official who has to spend large sums that he does not have to entertain his superiors must find some way of meeting this expense. As we have seen, district officials often raise money from merchants and others for official projects, and it would be surprising if some of the money were not used for entertainment expenses. Moreover, an official is frequently asked to bend a regulation for someone's convenience or profit, and in such a situation, a gift to (say) "the fund for the repair of the provincial offices" can induce the official to give the case special consideration.

The need to show proper respect for a superior also affects the work of the district officials adversely. When the officer calls one of them into his office, the latter drops whatever he is doing and goes at once. He would almost never think of replying that he was in the middle of an important piece of work and would go as soon as possible. This can lead to inconvenience for citizens in their contact with the officials as the following example shows.

One day in Central District, a woman came to the Registration Section to enter the names of her sons in the household register. She was told that she would have to show certain documents which she had not brought with her. That meant she would have to return the following day. She asked to make an appointment with the deputy district officer in charge of registration, but he told her that he could not make an appointment. He said that she should come any timeñ for, he was almost always in his office. When I asked him later why he could not make an appointment, he responded that he was afraid that the district officer might call him at the time of his appointment. If that happened he would have to go, and then he would miss his appointment which would be discourteous. So, he preferred to make no appointments. This view is widely shared among district officials responding to the survey: 99 percent of them said that when a superior called it was important for a subordinate to go immediately even if he was in the middle of a difficult piece of work.

The inability to ask a superior to wait is a fairly serious problem, because in order to build the people's trust the district office tries hard to make their business there as convenient as possible. As we have seen, officials frequently bend the rules and even break them in order to make someone's business more convenient. But much of the good will gained in these ways may be dissipated when citizens have to wait for long periods at the district office to see officials who refuse to make appointments.

In sum, an official who fails to display the proper respect for his superiors will make a poor impression on them which may nullify his other efforts to earn their trust. So, he takes special care to show respect, even if it involves him in corruption or hurts his work by taking up time with elaborate receptions or forces him to give poor service to citizens.

Maintaining Good Communications

The reader will recall that Thai provincial administrators lack staff assistants and that this lack makes it difficult for them to keep track of the field work of their subordinates. An official who understands this can build good relations with his superiors quite effectively by making a special effort to keep them informed. Thus, for example a deputy district officer from an outlying district who must go to the provincial office on business will often take the occasion to call on the governor.

91

This will give the governor an opportunity to find out about the progress of work at the outlying district. He will be grateful for opportunities of this sort, and officials who prove themselves to be reliable informants can build good personal relations with him in this way. Provincial section chiefs are similarly grateful for information. Moreover, an official who has done interesting work can use his visits to describe it to his superiors. Accomplishments which might fail to be noticed can be brought dramatically to the attention of higher officials who thus learn to associate the name and face of a particular subordinate with the accomplishments he has reported.

Just as the second and third grade officials visit the province to keep their superiors informed and to have a chance to bring accomplishments to their notice, so the first grade officials visit their departments in the central administration for the same purpose. In the words of one district officer,

> . . . the question is, how can you get your superior at the departmental level to see the results of your work? He is the one who can reward you. It depends on the technique of each person. The director general is in the Department of Local Administration. He doesn't know what every district officer is doing. I think that sometimes you have to go to visit him. You have to go and report.
>
> Perhaps when you go to the Ministry on official business, you can go and report the results of the work you have done. He may believe you or he may not. If he doesn't he may say, "This guy talks a lot," and send someone out to see whether you have really done what you said. It depends on the technique of each person in publicizing his work so that his superiors know about it.

In addition to visiting his superiors with reports, a clever official may invite them to view the progress of his work in field, as the district officer of Central District invited the governor of Northern Province to attend one of the village visits. Inviting the superior out to visit a project may provide the opportunity to reward him in other ways as well. One deputy district officer said,

92

TABLE 5.2

PERCENTAGE OF DISTRICT OFFICIALS PREFERRING TO
CONSULT SUPERIORS OR COLLEAGUES CONCERNING
PROBLEMS WITH WORK

Preferred Consultant	Respondent		
	Local Administration Official	Technical Section Head	All Sections
(A) District Officer	77%	33%	48%
(B) Provincial Superior	--	41	27
(C) (A) + (B)	77	74	75
(D) Colleague (deputy district officer or section head)	23	27	25

When the work is progressing, I come
and tell (the district officer). Then, he can
go and help. That way the people can see that
he is interested in them. It is not just that
I am. For, now all the district officers. . .
want to promote development. So, they go and
join in the work in the field. When the work
is successful, they can take part of the
credit.

Another very important way in which officials
maintain good communications with their superiors
is through consulting them when problems arise.
When a district official has a problem in his work,
he is much more likely to go to his superior for
advice than he is to go to his colleagues, as Table
5.2 shows. By going to his superior with problems,
a Thai official increases his superior's trust in
him because it appears to the superior that this
official does not try to hid problems. During the
observational phase of this research such consultation was often observed, and many officials spon-

taneously mentioned it as a good way of building personal relations with superiors. Of the district officials responding to the survey, 96 percent agreed that consultation was indeed a good way of building such personal relations.

Thai consultation practices are quite different from those reported by Blau (1963:127). His respondents were reluctant to discuss problems with their superior because they felt that it would make them appear to be unable to solve their own problems. Consequently, they preferred to consult their colleagues. Thai district officials discuss problems with their colleagues, of course, but they prefer to discuss them with superiors in order to build their trust.

The difference between the Thai and the American officials in their consultation patterns may be explained by the difference between the two groups in the distribution of authority. In the American setting, the subordinate official had a great deal of independent responsibility and was evaluated on the results of his work. In the Thai setting in contrast, the subordinate has very little authority It is closely held by the district officer who is officially responsible for everything that is done by his subordinates. Therefore, in the Thai setting, a trustworthy official does not take a risky decision without informing his superior and asking his advice.

The Thai situation is also very different from that of French officials. Crozier (1964:44-47) reported that in the clerical agency he studied, superiors found it virtually impossible to get reliable information on which to base decisions. The reason was that subordinates were so well protected by seniority regulations that their careers could not be influenced by their superiors. Consequently, the subordinates had no incentive to serve as channels of information. This contrast with the Thai situation serves to support my explanation of the reasons for the behavior of the Thai officials.

The patterns of consultation among district officials also reveal the effects of the division of power between the district officer and the technical section heads at the province. Table 5.2 shows the proportions of officials who said that they usually consulted one or another source of advice. Clearly, the majority of officials consult superiors more often than colleagues, as row (C)

94

of the table shows. The technical section heads, however, were divided over whether to consult the district officer or their provincial superiors, with more preferring the latter. In contrast, the Local Administration officials always consulted th district officer rather than their provincial superior. This pattern reflects the fact that the technical section heads give more importance than the deputy district officers do to building the trust of their provincial superiors, and that in turn reflects the ambiguity in the division of power between them and the district officer.

WORK AND SOCIAL EXCHANGE AMONG COLLEAGUES

Colleagueship Within the District Office

We now turn to a discussion of social exchange among colleagues. A District official needs to develop good collegial relations in order to be able to <u>amnuaj k'wamsaduag</u> for citizens as the quotation on page   shows. Collegial relations have been little studied in Thai society, and most researchers appear to have believed them unimportant. Wilson's (1962:116) description of the character of Thai political organizations is typical:

> The foundation of political life in Thailand is the clique, with a leader as the nucleus. A clique is fundamentally a face-to-face group because the characteristic ties binding it together are personal in nature-- ties of personal love and loyality based on the relationship between the leader and the follower. It would appear that there is a strong tendency for these ties to direct themselves up and down while lateral ties among the followers within the clique are not necessarily very strong.

Siffin appears to agree that egalitarian relationships are not terribly important in Thai social organization and inthe bureaucracy in particular. He says (1966:115) that superiority-subordination is "the essential basis for the posture of interpersonal relations" in Thailand. Other analysts appear to concur with this conclusion. Suvanajata (1973:473) says that hierarchical relations are more important than egalitarian relations in Thai society, and Wichaidit (1973:202) says that

95

egalitarian relationships are very difficult for
Thai people. Hanks and Phillips (1961:642) go so
far as to say that in Thai society, "... group co-
herence depends on status inequality. It is difficult for an equal to give anything of value to an
equal or to command his respect." Thus, the assumption appears to be that the detailed institu-
tionalization of superior-subordinate relations and
the widespread use of the elder sibling-younger
sibling (p'i-nɔng) forms of address to order informal relations leave little room for egalitarian interaction. This assumption has led to the neglect
of the study of the role of informal collegial relations in Thai organization.

My argument is that, as the pressure for performance in development work has increased, Thai
officials, like people in organizations elsewhere,
have felt a new need for collegial ties. That is
based on the fact that when men work in organizations their efforts must somehow be coordinated if
their joint tasks are to be accomplished, especially
when the tasks are as complex as those involved in
rural development. Coordination of activity in organizations is typically achieved in one of two
ways. In the classic "bureaucratic" organization
of the weberian model, it is achieved by a rigid
division of labor combined with a strict hierarchi-
calization of authority. Communication is expected
to be vertical, and coordination of the work of officials at the same level is achieved by referring
problems up the hierarchy until the individuals involved reach a common superior. This was the pattern developed in Thailand under Rama V and was
typical of Thai administration until recently
(Siffin, 1966:191).[5] The other method of coordination is through informal horizontal communication
among individuals whose expertise or resources are
needed for the solution of problems at hand. When
this sort of solution is formally adopted it takes
the form of "project organization" (Burns and Stalker, 1961:83-88). However, even when project organization does not exist, this solution may be adopted
by bureaucrats informally if pressure for performance is placed on them (e.g., Dalton, 1959:19-68)

It has been shown (Thompson, 1967:13; Hall,
1962:302; Burns and Stalker, 1961:121) that the
rigid, bureaucratic style of coordination is appropriate for organizations engaged in uniform and
easily routinized tasks, while the more flexible
style is appropriate for organizations whose tasks
are less uniform or less easily routinized. Organi-

zations that are faced with nonuniform or unroutin- izeable tasks and that insist rigidly on maintaining a strictly bureaucratic form of control will suffer a relative loss of effectiveness. Therefore, we can expect that in an organization where strong pressures for effective tasks performance exist low level officials will organize a substantial amount of informal horizontal coordination among themselves even if the formal organizational structure does not permit it. Such informal coordination of work among colleagues typically takes the form of social exchange as has frequently been observed (Blau, 1963; Dalton, 1959; Goffman, 1961).

Rural development work is, it will be agreed, both complex and difficult to routinize. To be successful it required flexible adaptation of pro- cedures by field officials. Therefore, if the theory outlined above is correct, "bureaucratic" administration of rural development programs is pos- sible only at a considerable cost in effectiveness, and any increase in effectiveness in organizations so administered is likely to be accompanied by an increase in horizontal coordination, either through the use of project organization or through informal social exchange among colleagues.

At Central District, such informal social ex- change has emerged around the officials' need for resources for development projects. Development officials who want the trust of citizens cannot amnuaj k'wamsaduag for them at district offices without the help of colleagues who provide the ser- vices that citizens want. For example, if a citi- zen goes to the district office to register the birth of a son, only a registration official can help him, but the registration official has little to gain from helping hi-. So, ordinarily the citi- zen will go to a development official who he knows, the public health officer perhaps, and will ask him for help. Then, the public health officer must ask a registration official for assistance. He will generally receive it as a favor to a colleague, and the citizen will go away happy, but the health offi- cer will have contracted a social debt. Responses to the survey indicate that this sort of request to a colleague is quite common; 95 percent of the dis- trict officials had had occasions to ask colleagues to expedite work for citizens.

The principles of reciprocity and equity in social exchange (Walster etc. al, 1973) as well as

97

ethnographic reports of Thai society (Piker, 1968: 778; Phillips, 1970:85) should lead us to expect that in order to obtain such assistance, officials would have to offer something in return, and indeed this is the case. As one development official said,

> When (other officials) have a lot of work to do, I help them if I have time. I offer to do typing for them or to give advice or to help them in some other way.

The above quotation shows that one way that colleagues can help one another is by giving advice, and indeed they do so quite often. 91 percent of the survey respondents had had occasion to ask colleagues for advice. Among the district officials there was a substantial difference between the deputy district officers and the technical section heads in the frequency with which they asked colleagues for advice. 27 percent of the former group had done so "often" while only 10 percent of the latter group had asked for advice often. The reason for this pattern is that each of the section heads is the sole representative of his speciality at the district office. So, often there is no colleague to whom he can turn. In contrast, there are several (generally from four to seven) deputy district officers, and therefore they can help one another.
In fact, the deputy district officers form something of a solidary group whose members are loyal to one another. This loyalty was displayed in an incident at Central District. One of the deputy district officers, thinking to please his superior, arranged to have pictures taken at one of the district's important activities. Unfortunately, he neglected to specify a limit either to the number of pictures to be taken or to the amount to be paid the photographer. The latter took a great many pictures and submitted a very large bill. The district officer refused to allow the district's funds to be used to pay for the photos, and so the officer who had ordered them was stuck with the bill which a-mounted to a large portion of his monthly salary. He was saved when his fellow deputy district officers collected enough among themselves to share the expense equally. In this incident we can see expressed the solidarity of the deputy district officers. No similar solidarity was observed among the technical section heads.
However, it should not be assumed that the technical sections do not cooperate in their work.

98

On the contrary, such cooperation was often observed. For instance, the agriculture officer and the cooperatives officer form a natural group. Both the Cooperatives Department and the Agricultural Extension Department have programs of organizing groups of farmers, but because of the autarky that characterizes Thai formal administration, these programs have not been combined although in many respects they duplicate one another. At the district level, however, the officials must cooperate in order to succeed in their work.

Thus, for instance, the agricultural extension officer lacks the expertise to supervise the financial operations of his farmers' groups properly and for this purpose he calls on the cooperatives officer. The latter is glad to help because he sometimes needs the help of the agriculture man. This occurs because the cooperatives man is supposed to advise the members of his cooperatives concerning new crops, insecticides and farming methods, but in fact he knows little of these matters. Thus, one of the cooperatives bought a pump to provide water to permit the growing of a second annual rice crop. Since none of the members of the cooperatives had even grown a second crop so they needed advice, and the agriculture man was asked to come and help, which he did. Thus, by an exchange of assistance both officials were able to accomplish more than they would have otherwise.

Another way that officials can help one another is by filling in for each other in emergencies. An official may be given a special assignment by a superior or have personal business to take care of. As mentioned in the last chapter, Thai officials feel strongly that when a superior calls it is important to go immediately even if one is engaged in an important piece of work. This creates a serious problem for officials who deal with the public because it prevents them from providing service at predictable times. They solve this problem by asking colleagues to stand in for them. They are able to obtain the aid they need because the officials who serve the public are precisely those who serve the public are precisely those who are able to amnuaj k'wamsaduag for citizens.[6] Thus, we should not be surprised to find that 81 percent of the survey respondents had been asked by colleagues to fill in for them.

Another way that colleagues can help one another is when large projects need to be done. This generally occurs when a deputy district officer is

99

given the responsibility of assembling a team for
some large task like supervising a village election.
In such a case, he must request the assistance of
the section chiefs because there are not enough deputy district officers to do the job. Occasions of
this sort were observed fairly frequently at Central District during the author's stay there, and
they given the technical section chiefs opportunities to return the favors of the deputy district
officers in helping to expedite villagers' business.

One might think that the deputy district officers who represent the district officer, would be
able to coerce the section chiefs even in the latter
had no particular reason to want to help. But in
fact the deputy district officers' power of coercion
is quite limited. The reason is that the division
of authority between the district officer and the
provincial section heads (See Figure 3.2) makes the
former's control over the district section heads
problematic. He must earn their loyalty in order to
be able to control them. So, he does not like to
force them to help unwillingly with the work of
Local Administration. Consequently, a deputy district officer must build good relations with the
heads of the technical sections in order to be able
to rely in their cooperation.

Social exchange among officials shades off into situations where official help is exchanged for
personal benefits. Thus, for instance one official
at Central District kept ducks to sell as commercial side line. In order to protect them from disease he asked the district veterinarian for help.
Although that gentleman was a civil official and
not a private practitioner, the officer who had the
ducks felt it politic to repay him. He said nothing at the time, but later the veterinarian received
a small share of the profits from the sale of the
ducks.

Exchange With Officials of Other Agencies

Exchange also takes place between the officials of the district and those of other agencies.
For example, the district's development programs require the use of heavy construction equipment that
the district does not possess, and such equipment
may be obtained from other agencies like the army or
the Accelerated Rural Development Program (ARD). In
its relationships with these agencies the district
exploits its monopoly of access to the villages.
The village headmen are subordinates of the district

100

officer, and their cooperation with the projects
of other agencies can ordinarily be obtained only
with his approval. The resulting social exchanges
were described by an official of Central District
in an interview:

> (Interviewer) As far as you have seen are
> the other agencies happy to help you, or
> do they feel that their own work is enough
> for them.

> (Respondent) It varies. If we are friends
> with them, that is if they have worked with
> us before, and the villagers gave them good
> cooperation, they want to come.

Thus, lateral social exchange has emerged
among officials in different agencies in response to
demands for effective performance.

Symbolic Gestures in Social Exchange

Social exchange like that described above is
normally not accomplished on a "cash and carry"
basis. That is, an ARD official, for example, does
not go to the district office and say, "I'll trade
you two days use of a dump truck for a letter to
the headman of Ban Dong village asking his cooperation with a project of ours." As has been discussed, social exchange is ordinarily oriented not
toward the direct exchange of equivalent values but
toward the maintenance of relationships within
which assistance may be obtained at need. In such
situations an actor must try to express by a wide
variety of symbolic gestures the fact that he is
conscious of his social debts and that he cares
about the relationship.

Among Thai officials, the most important forms
such gestures taken are invitations to eat or drink
and attendance at the merit making[7] ceremonies of
colleagues. These are traditional activities, but
they have been adapted to new purposes. A Thai
official who did not invite his friends out to eat
or attend their merit makings would be regarded as
stingy and would find himself gradually cut off
from the network of friendship in which assistance
is given. This is shown by the fact that 91 percent
of the survey respondents said that participation in
such activities was important for success in official work.

This instrumental use of conviviality appears to be an adaptation of a traditional Thai pattern to the solution of contemporary problems. Thai people have long been known for their love of conviviality, and Thai social life includes many formal and informal occasions for eating and drinking with freinds. In the past, this sociability appears to have been balued for its own sake (Siffin 1966: 162; Phillips, 1967:349-50). Joining with friends in such ways was not regarded as a way of indicating a willingness to provide more substantial assistance Now, however, the sociable occasions that are so prominent a feature of Thai life have taken on an instrumental value. An official treats his colleagues to lunch not merely as a gesture of respect or of liking, but in order to construct or to maintain useful relationships in which he will be able to obtain aid when he needs it. As one official said,

> I have that (drink with other officials) because I am in Local Administration. That sort of socializing is necessary, but if I do it too much my salary will be too little. So, I have to try to get the most out of the time I have in order to make the expense as small as possible.

The forms of interaction among officials at social events show another way that the traditional behavior of Thai officials has been altered by the need to establish and maintain collegial friendships. Thai society places great emphasis on displays of respect and deference by younger people to their seniors. Consequently, it is rare in Thailand to see people of widely differing ages drinking together. The formality required between people of different ages is too great to permit the sort of ribald conversation that alcohol encourages. However, at Central District it was quite common to see officials drinking together who were similar in rank but widely different in age. During such drinking, a minimum of formal recognition of age differences was maintained through the use of "p'i" (elder brother) as a form of address, but in other ways the informality appropriate to interaction among equals was displayed (e.g., by joking and by the use of vulgar language).

Similarly, the need for collegiality overrode the traditional norms of respect for age when a

young official of high educational attainment in-
teracted with an older official of a lower educational attainment in the work setting. This might
be a difficult situation because it presents the
actors with conflicting bases for deference. For
example, when social interaction occurs between a
33 year old official with a master's degree and a
41 year old official with a secondary school diploma
who is to pay respect to whom? In principle, respect is always paid to elders, and 96 percent of
the district respondents to the survey said that
they paid more respect to age than to education or
official status.

In practice, however, things are not so simple
What actually occurred at Central District was that
the younger man called the older "elder brother"
but did not use the respectful "k'rab"[8] while the
elder used "k'rab" in speaking to the younger. Thus,
each paid respect to the other in turn, and no
clear ascendency was established. No awkardness resulted from the lack of clarity in ranking between
these two officials, and it appeared to me that
they were able to work together quite comfortably.

In short, the forms of respect have taken on
a somewhat altered meaning. Traditionally, age was
the main basis of respect and deference, and the
use of the term "p'i" established an unambiguous
status hierarchy. How, however, age competes with
education as a basis for status claims, and the use
of the term "p'i" as a form of address does not imply acceptance of an inferior status to that of the
person addressed. Instead, it expresses no more
than that a certain claim to status has been recognized. Thus, it becomes possible (as it would not
have been before) for one addressed as "p'i" to say
"k'rab" to his junior out of respect for his education.

An official will make a special effort to be
respectful when he is asking another for assistance,
especially if the latter is outside of the department of the official who needs help. One does not
simply call up a colleague in another agency to ask
him for help; a visit is made to his office or home.
Such a visit has a definite form. When one official visits another, the host will receive him with
great formality. A clerk will be sent out for coffee, and small talk engaged in until it arrives. One
of the officials will offer the other a cigarette.
They will sip their coffee. Only then will the host
ask a visitor about the object of his visit, and the

latter will make his request. These visits are
quite time consuming, and officials frequently complain of their necessity, but no one would wish to
seem to fail in respect for his colleagues.

However, officials who are friends, either because they have worked together in the past or because they became acquainted elsewhere, can often
dispense with visits of this sort. If one needs
the other's help, he simply calls the other on the
telephone. This means that it is much more convenient to work with friends than with others. So,
relatively stable informal networks emerge. One of
the important bases for such networks is graduation
from the same university, especially in the same
class. Thus, for example, when one deputy district
officer wanted some blankets to distribute to poor
villagers during village visits, he simply called
the provincial welfare officer and asked for them.
He said that he could do that because the welfare
officer had been his classmate in college.

Graduation from the same university does not,
by itself, provide more than a minimal basis for a
relationship, however. There are not very many universities in Thailand; so, a large proportion of
one's colleagues are likely to share one's alma
mater. However, when two officials from the same
school meet, they immediately have a topic of conversation, and they may also have mutual friends.
So, it is easier to build a relationship with a person from one's university. If the person graduated
in the same class, then the chances are one knows
him already, and in any case classmates are supposed
to help each other.

The two most prestigious universities,
Chulalongkorn and Thammasat, have active alumni
associations in Northern Province, and they sponsor
social activities for their members. This increases
the chance that graduates of the same university
will get to know each other. In the case of
Chulangkorn University, there is also another factor
The students of Chula maintain a strong tradition of
mutual assistance between older and younger students
The latter are supposed to defer to their seniors,
and they are supposed to help and protect their
juniors. This tradition is carried on through life,
and so alumni of Chula always have a network of fellow alumni on whom they can call for assistance.

However, one should not overestimate the importance of these alumni networks. For, it often
happens that an official must ask for assistance

104

from someone who is not an _alumnus_ of his school,
and the longer an official has been out of school,
the more opportunity he has had to build friendships on other bases. Nevertheless, "old boy" networks do play a significant role.

CONCLUSIONS

    In this chapter we have seen that certain im-
portant structural features of the Thai civil service cause district officials to build their roles
in certain ways. The cumbersome and unstandardized
evaluation system of the Thai civil service and the
centralization of reward power force officials to
concentrate their efforts on dramatic projects with
highly visible results in order to bring their work
to the attention of overloaded decision makers far
above them in the hierarchy. These same factors
force officials to give special efforts to avoiding
conspicuous failures, even to the extent of using
their own money or of working overtime without extra pay to get work done on time. However, failures
that are unlikely to be detected are not avoided,
as is shown by the fact that little effort is given
to assuring the accuracy of statistics given in reports.
    We have also seen how the above factors, to-
gether with the political structure of Thailand,
led officials to raise resources locally, although
it was illegal for them to do so. Moreover, raising resources involved officials in social exchange
with citizens in which services that were supposed
to be available universalistically to all were in
fact given preferentially to those who had helped
or might help with the district's development work.
In addition, officials engaged in various illegal
activities like permitting tax evasion and cutting
trees in protected forests.
    Another important structural feature of the
situation of the district officials was the lack of
advisory staff at the provincial and departmental
levels of administration. This lack provided an
opportunity for officials to build their relations
with superiors by making themselves into channels
of information. This was done not only directly but
also indirectly through consultation with superiors.
The patterns of consultation also revealed the division of power between the district officer and the
provincial heads of technical sections.
    In addition, we have seen that the cultural

emphasis on extreme respect for superiors caused officials to act in ways which had undesirable consequences in order to obtain the trust of their superiors. The need to go immediately when the superior called was shown to interfere with the goal of providing convenient service to citizens. The requirement of respect also led to the giving of large, constly receptions for visiting superiors, and this in turn was one factor leading to corruption.

The culturally sanctioned diffuseness of official roles also had consequences in the behavior of officials. It led them to make themselves available to perform various unofficial personal services for their superiors. However, not all officials availed themselves equally of the opportunity to build relations with their superiors in this way. For some, the sense of accomplishment to be gained from doing good work was important enough that advancement obtained by "going in the back of the house" was unsatisfying. Besides regularly working overtime, officials also made an effort to visit their superiors at home in order to place themselves at the superiors' disposal. This would appear strange in the American cultural context, but in Thailand it appeared quite natural.

We have also seen that Thai officials have altered traditional patterns of interaction in response to the demands of development. The overwhelmingly vertical orientation that characterized traditional Thai administration has been supplemented by the more flexible horizontal ties required by rural development work. The need for coordination in the use of resources for development has created a situation in which it is no longer "difficult for an equal to give anything of value to any equal," and therefore new sorts of relationships have emerged among the officials of the district office and between them and officials of other agencies.

Consistent with these new relationships is the increasing egalitarianism in the symbolic forms of interaction among officials. This is evidenced by the use of "k'rab" from an older official to a younger and by the fact that colleagues of widely different ages can drink together comfortably. The new egalitarianism also appears in the fact that the old, respectful use of "p'i" as a form of address no longer connotes a definite subordination as it once did.

We also find a change in the meaning of traditional gestures of fellowship. Eating and drinking

106

together and attendance at merit makings, which
used to be valued for their own sakes, have become
symbolic gestures that are used to maintain relationships in the context of which other sorts of
favors may be asked. Although the meanings of such
gestures change, they do not change very rapidly.
It is necessary for them to be reasonably stable
because they are a conventional language. If they
changed too rapidly, they could not be used for
communication because they would be incomprehen-
sible. Thus, attending a person's merit making is
now, as in the past, an expression of friendship
(although the meaning of friendship may have
changed), and if it did not have this meaning it
could not be understood as a gesture. Strictly
symbolic behavior changes more slowly than other
sorts of behavior and lends a sense of stability to
actors in a changing scene.

NOTES

     1. The material in this section first appeared
in a slightly different form in my paper, "Clientelism and Rural Development in Thailand," Rural
Sociology 43.
     2. Much of the material in this section and
the next two first appeared in a somewhat abrevi-
ated form in my paper, "Clientelism and Rural Development in Thailand," Rural Sociology 43.
     3. The finding that peasants and officials
engage in social exchange of this specific sort is
somewhat different from Rubin's (1973) finding that
peasants felt a sense of awe toward officials and
felt that they could not reciprocate officials'
favors adequately. It is true that villagers preferred projects to be organized by officials, as
Rubin says, but this should not surprise us. In
every society, development is spearheaded by the
educated class, and in rural Thailand the educated
class is composed almost entirely of officials.
     4. A businessman might, of course, purchase
the good will of the revenue officer directly by
bribes, but this would be less satisfactory for two
reasons. First, the district officer can do more
for a merchant than the revenue officer can because
the district officer's authority is broader. Second, a donation to the support of a local development project brings honor as well as wealth and convenience, and a bribe could not accomplish so much.
     5. This does not, of course, imply that there
were no differences between the weberian model and

Thai administrative practice.

6. For the sake of simplicity of exposition, I have ignored the fact that some deputy district officers are also development officials. Exchanges among the deputy district officers are similar to those between them and the section chiefs.

7. "Merit making" is a part of Buddhist religious practice. On important occasions, Thai people perform ritual acts regarded as meritorious, and this usually involves providing meal for a group of monks. Attending such a ceremony at a friends home and sharing in the cost of the ceremony are regarded as ways of honoring the friend.

8. There is no English equivalent to "k'rab." It is a word which is used at the ends of sentences to express respect for the person addressed.

6. The Physicians and Their Situation

In the preceding chapters, we have seen how the conduct of district officials is affected by various structural and cultural properties of its setting. In this chapter, we will begin an examination of the behavior of physicians in provincial hospitals in Thailand. The structural setting of medical work is quite different from that of district administration in several ways. Specifically, the structure of incentives facing physicians is quite different from that which faces administrative officials, and the distribution of power in a hospital is very different from that in a district office. In addition there are cultural differences between physicians and district officials. The former subscribe to professional norms of autonomy, collegiality, and commitment to technical proficiency that the district officials do not share or at least share to a lesser degree. These differences in the structural and cultural properties of the two situations lead to significantly different patterns of behavior by the two groups of officials.

The effect of these differences is that physicians have much less need to earn the trust of their superiors than district officials do, and consequently they put much less effort into earning it. Physicians must maintain a certain minimal level of performance in order to avoid censure, but beyond that their power and professional autonomy leave them free to do more or less as they please. They use this freedom to engage in private medical practice to augment their incomes, but at the same time they do not leave the civil service. So, reconciling the demands of private practice with those of public service becomes a basic problem in Thai medical life. This

chapter will compare the structural position of
physicians to that of district officials and will
describe the character of Thai medical professionalism. The following chapter will analyze the
behavior of Thai physicians and compare it to that
of district officials.

Riverton Hospital, where medical practice was
observed, is a modern building in downtown Riverton,
the capital of River Province. Riverton is a major
trading center in the northern region of Thailand,
and the town also has some small industry. However, most of River Province's three-quarters of a
million people are engaged in **agriculture** and rice
is the most important **crop**.

Riverton Hospital is modern and well equipped
by the standards of rural Thailand. Its surgical
facilities are adequate for most kinds of surgery
except brain or open heart surgery. Its medical
facilities are somewhat less adequate because of
a shortage of laboratory equipment and technicians
which renders some diagnostic procedures impracti-
cal. In general, the shortage of staff is a much
more serious limitation than any lack in the
equipment. The hospital has about 375 beds which
are usually full and a large clinic where outpatient services are provided during official hours
from 8 A.M. to 4 P.M. Monday through Friday and in
the morning on Saturday. The hospital also has an
emergency room which provides emergency medical and
surgical services at all times. The hospital is
staffed by a director who is a physician, sixteen
physicians engaged in patient care, about sixty
general nurses[1] and practical nurses, and a somewhat larger number of nurse-aides and orderlies.

Inpatients at Riverton receive care in four
departments which are Internal Medicine, Surgery,
Pediatrics, and Obstetrics-Gynecology. The physicians are distributed among the departments as
follows:

    Internal Medicine: 4
    Surgery: 6
    Pediatrics: 2
    Obstetrics and Gynecology: 4

Each department has two inpatient wards with between 80 and 120 patients to care for at any one
time. Each physician cares for inpatients only
in his department.

In the outpatient clinic, there is less specialization than in the inpatient department. Every effort is made to direct each patient to a doctor of the appropriate specialty, but the number of medical patients is much greater than the number of patients of any other type. So, the internists cannot possibly see them all, and many of them are seen by doctors in other departments. Consequently, everyone is a general pactitioner in the clinic.

Riverton Hospital is the regular government hospital in River Province and belongs to the Ministry of Public Health. The organizational relationship between the hospital and the Ministry has undergone a good deal of change recently and is still rather fluid. At the moment[2] the hospital belongs to the Office of the Undersecretary of the Ministry. The representative of the Office in the province is the chief medical officer (naj p'aed jaj) who is the subordinate of the governor and the immediate superior of the director of the hospital. However, the director is himself a first or special grade officer and is accustomed to dealing directly with the governor and with the central administration of his department. So, the chief medical officer has little importance in the hospital.

THE DISTRIBUTION OF POWER IN THE HOSPITAL

Under the regulations of the Ministry of Public Health, the distribution of authority in the hospital is not very different from that of the district office. Formal authority rests with the director, and others must in theory follow his orders. However, in reality the position of the director of the hospital is much weaker than that of the district officer.

The power of the district officer is based on the fact that he can withhold or delay approval of his subordinates' proposals for their work. In addition, he may also be able to help his subordinates to advance in their careers by recommending them for double raises, and advancement is very important to district officials. Finally, the district officials cannot openly defy the district officer because to do so would be to risk expulsion from the civil service.

The situation of the physicians is different from that of the district officials on all three of these dimensions. The hospital director has

very few occasions to approve proposals from his
physicians. Their work consists for the most part
of patient care, and because of the norm of professional autonomy, an order for medication or a
decision to do surgery does not have to be approved
by the director. The incentive system of the civil
service is much less effective in motivating physicians than it is in motivating district officials
for reasons which will be discussed below, and
therefore the director has relatively little to
offer the physicians. Finally, a physician does
not need the civil service as much as it needs him.
He can make a living in private practice, but the
shortage of doctors in Thailand makes the director
very reluctant to lose him. Consequently, the
power of the physicians is much greater than that
of the district civil servants.

In addition to these structural factors,
professional norms of autonomy and collegiality
prevent the director of the hospital from behaving
in a dictatorial manner. Professional norms
function to limit his exercise of authority both
because they legitimate a staff member's refusal to
obey an order and because the director is a physician himself and believes in the importance of
professional autonomy. The chain of command of
the Ministry of Public Health supports the director
and the staff physicians in their adherence to
professional norms of autonomy and collegiality
because virtually everyone of any importance in
that hierarchy is a physician. Although I have
not made a thorough study, I believe it is fair
to say that in the Ministry of Public Health no
physician is ever placed under the authority of
someone who is not a physician. This does not mean
that there are no gradations of authority in the
Ministry, but it does mean that a superior there
is less powerful than he would be in other ministries. To give a simple example, the Ministry of
Public Health rarely transfers a physician from
one hospital to another without first asking him if
he wants to be transferred. This is in contrast
to the policies of the other ministries which simply
issue orders. For all these reasons, the physician
is much more independent in his work than the
district official. The doctor does not need to
earn autonomy because he already has a great deal
of it, and the director must accept the fact that
there are things he cannot compel his staff to do.

112

THE INCENTIVES OF THE PHYSICIANS

Formal Incentives

In order to understand the behavior of the physicians, we must know something of the incentives they face. As mentioned, the doctors are regular, full-time civil servants, and they receive the regular civil service salaries which we know are inadequate. As a group, physicians are better paid than most officials (see Table 6.1), because on the average they are of higher grade. In addition, most doctors have comfortable houses provided for them on the grounds of their hospitals. So, in principle they could live on their salaries. Moreover, the civil service provides a professional career ladder for them which means that a physician can be promoted in grade as soon as he has passed the promotional examination and does not have to wait for a vacant position. A physician can rise to the first grade and sometimes to the special grade without ever carrying administrative responsibility. Finally, in recognition of the long training required of physicians, the civil service allows them to enter at the second grade instead of at the third grade with other holders of bachelor's degrees.[3] However, according to the measure used here physicians are at least as dissatisfied with their remuneration as are other officials, as Table 6.1 shows.

TABLE 6.1
Salaries and Desired Incomes (In Baht) of Physicians and District Officials and Index of Dissatisfaction with Salaries

	Mean Desired Income (A)	Mean Salary (B)	Index of Dissatisfaction (A) ÷ (B)
Physicians	11,141	4150	2.68
District Officials	4192	2161	1.94

The difference between the indices of dissatisfaction of the two groups is not significant at $\alpha = .05$.

113

Moreover, while it is true that physicians may be promoted more easily than district officials, it is not true that rewards come regularly to those who do good work. On the contrary, good work is not consistently rewarded unless it is combined with political skill. Just as at the district, a doctor must bring his work to the attention of his superiors and build personal relations with them in order to be rewarded.

However, unlike district officials, most physicians do not try very hard to build good relations with their superiors because they have a much more lucrative alternative, namely private medical practice outside of official hours. Table 6.2 shows that the majority of Thai physicians moonlight and that in this they differ from district officials. The incomes received from private medical practice are very large--five or ten times as large as official salaries according to the physicians at Riverton. If they were to practice privately full time, they would presumably earn even more, but they prefer to remain in the civil service. This means that it must offer substantial informal rewards, and to these we now turn our attention.

Informal Incentives

In many ways the physicians' reasons for preferring to remain in the civil service are similar to those of the district officials, as a comparison of Table 6.3 with Table 4.2 will show. The security, fringe benefits, and prestige of the civil service make it attractive to both groups as does the opportunity it offers for advancement. In the case of the last named item, however, it is probable that, while the response rates of the two groups are quite similar, the meanings of their responses differ. There are two reasons for this: first, the objective opportunity offered for advancement is greater for the physicians than for the district officials. The average length of time in the service of the physicians surveyed was 12.7 years, and most of them were first grade officials, while the district officials surveyed had an average seniority of 19.2 years, and among them only the district officers had reached the first grade. So, physicians have more advancement to be satisfied with.

114

TABLE 6.2

Proportion of Physicians and of District Officials who Moonlight

	Proportion Who Moonlight	Proportion Who Do Not Moonlight	Total
Physicians	67%	33%	100% (49)
District Officials	38	62	100 (76)

t = 2.60   df = 4   α < .05

The second reason is that working in a hospital can help a physician to establish a private medical practice. The physicians at Riverton explained to me that a part of the proper strategy for starting a successful private practice was to work for a time in the hospital in order to become known. This being so, it follows that not all of the advancement available to a civil service physician is in the civil service.

It is interesting that the physicians named the prestige of the civil service as an important reason for preferring it to other careers because this response is contrary to a prediction made before carrying out the survey. I predicted that the prestige of the civil service would be less important to physicians than to district officials on the grounds that the former would, as in the United States, identify themselves primarily as physicians rather than as civil servants. In fact, however, the data show that if anything the reverse is true: 38 percent of the physicians gave the prestige of the civil service as a reason for preferring it to private occupations as compared with only 28 percent of the district officials.

An article by Maxwell (1975) throws light on possible reasons for the emergence of this pattern in the data. Maxwell shows, using Weber's theoretical categories, that old Thailand's elite was patrimonial rather than feudal. A patrimonial elite, because of its openness, tends to absorb new groups as they rise while a feudal elite tends to

TABLE 6.3
Reasons for Preferring the Civil Service Over Other Occupations: Physicians

	Percentage of Physicians Saying That a Reason Was for Them:			
	(A) Most Im-portant	(B) 2nd Most Im-portant	(C) 3rd Most Im-portant	Either (A), (B) or (C)
The civil service gives me a chance to use my knowledge and skill.	52*	10	10	72
The civil service offers great security.	22	24	16	62
The civil service offers good fringe benefits.	6	20	26	52
Society accords high prestige to a civil servant.	6	12	20	38
The civil service offers good opportunity for advancement.	—	28	10	38

*The columns do not total to 100% because items chosen by very few respondents have been ommitted. The right hand column totals to more than 100% because each respondent made three ranked choices.

exclude rising groups and therefore to produce competing sources of prestige. At the same time, the patrimonial state tends to absorb into itself as many social functions as possible and thus creates positions for rising technical elites during periods of economic development. Maxwell's analysis is consistent with the data from this study which show that 56 percent of the physicians are the sons of merchants, a rising group in Thai society. This example illustrates well the importance of understanding fully the unique constellation of historical forces in a society in order to be able to apply the general principles of science to the explanation of the behavior of the society's members.

To return to the data, the most important difference between the incentive patterns of physicians and those of district officials is the relatively greater importance given by physicians to the item, "The civil service gives me a chance to use my knowledge and skill." Nearly three-fourths of the physicians chose this item, and a majority chose it as the most important reason for preferring a civil service career to one in private practice. The popularity of this item reflects the doctors' professional commitment to careers using their technical skills.

A physician who really wants to use and maintain his skills is almost forced to choose a civil service career. For, only a full-time civil servant may care for inpatients in a state hospital, and the overwhelming majority of the hospitals belong to the state.[4] The fact that so many physicians remain in the civil service in spite of the low salaries it offers is therefore an expression of medical professionalism. The physicians' desire to be able to use their technical skills also appeared in interviews conducted at Riverton. In response to open ended questions, the doctors frequently mentioned the opportunity to use skills as a reason for remaining in the civil service. Thus, it is no exaggeration to say that the drama of Thai medical practice lies in the conflict between professionalism and profitability.

THE PROFESSIONALISM OF THE THAI PHYSICIAN

Professionalism is a concept which is meaningful in Western societies, but is it useful for understanding behavior in Thai society? In old

117

Thailand there were no independent, professional groups. The unitary, hierarchical, and autocratic society of that period left no room for associations whose standards and authority were independent in principle from those of the throne (Rabibhadana, 1969:97ff). However, the modernization of the kingdom in the twentieth century has included the establishment of Western style schools of law, medicine, engineering, education, and nursing. These schools have of necessity been staffed by Westerners and by Thais trained in the West. They have inculcated in their students not only the skills of their respective professions but also the professional ideals of commitment to technical proficiency and to disinterested service which are the normative basis of professional work and the ideals of autonomy and collegiality which form the normative basis of professional association in the West.

Some of these norms have taken root easily in Thai society, and some have not. The notion of commitment to service is not restricted to professionals. As has been shown, Thai society already possesses norms of public service which come from Buddhism. In addition, the modernization ideals, as Myrdal (1968:57) has called them, include a commitment to national development and to improved public welfare. Accordingly, the Thai physician's belief in service includes both the standard professional commitment to the welfare of his patients and also a commitiment to the welfare of his country or sometimes of his community. The professional ideal of technical proficiency is a strong one among Thai physicians as we have shown. Most of the members of the staff of Riverton demonstrated this in various ways: they followed up interesting cases; they carried on teaching and research in the hospital; and they took time to obtain advanced training abroad.

Autonomy in professional work is also a strong norm among Thai physicians. When one of the department heads at Riverton was asked whether he checked the charts of patients under the care of his subordinates in order to be sure that proper care was being given, he answered, "By medical custom we do not do that." The strength of the norm of professional autonomy is also supported by data from the survey. Table 6.4 shows that physicians very rarely need to obtain the approval of their superior in order to carry out work they have planned. This is contrary to the usual pattern of

118

centralization of decision making which is a widespread and deeply engrained feature of Thai offi-
cialdom, and therefore the very large difference
between the physicians and the district officials
on this item indicates that medical professionalism
is quite firmly established.

Collegiality is more problematic. In the
sense of collegial administration, it is strong at
Riverton because it serves the needs of the physicians and because bureaucratic administration
would be very difficult in the face of the weak
position of the director. The prevalence of the
collegial style of administration is supported by
the survey responses shown in Table 6.5. The data
give moderate support to the prevalence of collegial administration among Thai physicians. The
difference between them and the district officials
on this item is not significant at the .05 level,
but the trend is in the direction predicted, and
it is quite strong.

Collegiality is weakened among Thai physicians
by the weakness of the organizational basis of
their of professional solidarity. There is a Thai
Medical Association, but only about half of the
physicians in Thailand are members, and there are
no local medical associations in the provinces.
The only place where all of the physicians in a
province (including those working for the Department of Public Health as well as the few private
physicians) can meet is the Chulalongkorn University Alumni Association which, of course, includes people who are not physicians.

TABLE 6.4
Freedom to Work Without Seeking the Approval of a Superior

Before carrying out a piece of work I have planned, I must
obtain my superior's approval:

	Always	Usually	Seldom	Never	Total
Physicians	–	–	15%	85%	100% (48)
District Officials	36%	44%	19	1	100% (78)

t = 19.994	df = 4	α < .0005

119

TABLE 6.5
Work Assignment by Staff Discussion Vs. Work Assignment by
Executive Order

Is the assignment of duties to physicians (officials) discussed in staff meetings or does the director (district
officer) make the decision himself?

	Discussed in Meetings	Superior Decides	Total
Physicians	73%	27%	100% (48)
District Officials	39%	61%	100% (75)

N.S. at $\alpha = .05$

Professional solidarity is also eroded by
competition for private patients. Several physicians reported to me examples of competitive behavior contrary to medical ethics. For example, it
was not uncommon for one doctor to criticize to
patients the knowledge or ability of another. One
physician who had been trained in the United States
said that a competitor of his had told some patients that he (my informant) was an expert in the
care of American patients but not of Thai patients.
When professional solidarity is weak, we can
expect that enforcement of professional standards
of practice will also be weak, and this is indeed
the case. Several types of malpractice were
reported to me, but no informant could remember
an occasion when a physician had been disciplined
by the Thai Medical Association for medical mal-
feasance. A few cases could be remembered in
which mild disciplinary measures had been taken
against physicians who had committed such clearly
illegal acts as signing false medical certificates
to enable friends to collect civil service sickness
benefits, but that was all.
The low level of professional solidarity of
Thai physicians is not surprising. The professions
of law and medicine which have strong solidary
organizations in the West have a long history of
corporate existence in a political environment composed of competing estates, classes, free munici-

palities, guilds, trade unions, and other sorts of interest groups. The political history of the West consists very largely of the conflicts among these groups, and as has been shown (Coser, 1956: 95; Scott, 1976:611) social conflict among groups produces solidarity within each of them. So, it is not surprising that the legal and medical associations should be as strong as they are in the West. Thai professional groups, on the other hand, have emerged very recently in the history of a country with no tradition of interest group conflict within the body politic (Wilson, 1962:232ff). So, it should not surprise us to find the professional solidarity of Thai physicians quite weak compared to that of physicians in Western countries.

In short, the professionalism of Thai physicians is strong in commitment to technical competence, to disinterested service and to individual autonomy in work, but it is weak in collegiality in the sense of professional solidarity. When it comes to collegiality as a style of administration, the data are ambiguous. The informal observations and interviews support the prevalence of collegial administration, and the trend of the survey data is in that direction, but the difference between the district officials and the physicians, while substantial, is not significant.

CONCLUSIONS

In this chapter I have given a general description of the work situation of the Thai physician in a provincial hospital and have discussed the major independent variables of this study. I have shown that, compared to district officials, physicians are very powerful. The power of the physicians is based both on their command of a scarce resource, namely their skill, from which they could easily earn a living outside of the civil service and on professional norms of autonomy and collegiality. The influence of professional norms is important, not only because the staff physicians believe in them but also because the director and other members of the hierarchy are physicians and support the staff in their commitment to professional standards.

I have also discussed the incentives of the physicians, observing that while they are relatively better paid than other civil servants, the gap between what the physicians earn in salaries and what they would like to earn is even greater for them than for the district officials. At the same time, the physicians say that the opportunity for advancement is an important reason for preferring the civil service to full time private employment. In the light of the apparent contradiction between these two findings, it was suggested that, in part, the opportunity for advancement referred to by the physicians was the economic advancement which their official jobs would bring to their private practices.

An important difference between the incentive pattern of physicians and that of district officials was the importance that the physicians gave to the opportunity afforded by a civil service career for the exercise of their technical skills. The emphasis on this incentive was pointed to as an indicator of the professionalism of the physicians when compared to the district officials. Thai physicians were also seen to be highly committed to norms of service and autonomy. It appears that collegial administration is typical of Thai physicians and that in this they differ from the district officials, but the data do not permit us to be sure.

As will be seen in the following chapters, the effect of the strong position of the physicians and their dissatisfaction with the incentives offered them is that in general they do not try very hard to obtain advancement in the civil service. Instead, their work is motivated by professional norms and by a desire to build reputations that will help their private practices. However, engaging in private practice while at the same time holding an official position is difficult and involves the physicians in continual infractions of civil service regulations and medical norms. Several aspects of their behavior are heavily influenced by the need to resolve this dilemma, as will be described in Chapter Seven.

NOTES

1. General nurses in Thailand receive three and a half years of training, only one term less than an American R.N. One reason for giving nurses three and a half years of training instead of four is to keep their salaries down. If four years were required and a bachelor's degree awarded, nurses would enter the civil service at the third grade which would be very expensive for the state.

2.   In 1974 when this research was done.
3.   Thai medical schools, like those in Great Britain, give a degree of Bachelor of Medicine.
4.   Most of those that do not belong to the state are Christian missionary hospitals which, I was told, give preference in hiring and in promotion to Christian doctors. Most Thai doctors are Buddhists and do not want to change their religion.

7. Private Practice and Public Service

A DOCTOR'S DAY

A doctor at Riverton Hospital's Outpatient
Clinic sits all morning in a little cubicle through
the door of which a nurse admits patients one by
one to be examined and treated. As each patient
is admitted, he is asked a few simple questions and
examined briefly. The doctor works very quickly;
for, the patients are many.
Anyone observing the doctors at work in the
clinic can see that each one has a particular examination routine that bears little relationship to
the complaints the patients bring. Thus, for instance, one doctor always listens to the patient's
hearts or lungs with a stethoscope while another
never or rarely does. The patients' complaints are,
for the most part, equally routine. An enormous
proportion of the patients come with a small number
of readily indentifiable diseases. For example,
gastrointestinal infections that result from drinking dirty water are very common in Thailand in the
dry season. So, an experienced physician seeing
his twentieth complaint of stomach pains and diar-
rhea on a hot day in April when no rain has fallen
for a month can guess the nature of the patient's
disease with a high probability of being correct.
Since he has, in any case, no time for a really
thorough examination, his behavior becomes ritu-
alized. He does something designed to express his
concern and to reassure the patient, and then he
prescribes some medication.
This routine is repeated over and over, dozens
of times each morning. Many people unfamiliar with
a physician's work have a romantic idea of it. They
see him as a valiant, humanitarian battling for

124

the lives of his patients. In fact, most of a
physician's time is spent in a mind numbing routine
that is both demanding and boring.

Moreover, the work load is very heavy. On an
average day, a physician in the Clinic at Riverton
sees a much larger number of patients than does a
physician in group practice in the United States as
the figure in Table 7.1 show. Most physicians at
Riverton also maintain private practices outside of
official hours. These private clinics generally
open at seven in the morning. So, a doctor arrives
at the hospital after having already seen a number
of patients. Naturally, under these circumstances
they have adopted strategies for reducing their
work load there.

Physicians at Riverton also care for inpatients,
but the setting and routine of inpatient care are
quite different from those of outpatient care.
First, the patients in a ward are not strangers.
The doctor has seen all of them more than once except for one or two new patients who may have been
admitted during the night. So, he is interested in
them and in their problems. Secondly, the patients
in a ward are generally quite sick and give the
doctor a chance to exercise his technical skills
which, as we saw in the last chapter, are important
to him. A third factor is that, contrary to what
one might expect, most of the patients in a ward
do not require much of the doctor's attention. The
reason is that once a patient's condition has been
diagnosed and the treatment begun the doctor has
only to monitor his condition to see that it im-
proves satsifactorily. It is only with new patients
or with those in whom the failure of a treatment
indicates the possibility of a misdiagnosis that
the doctor must work carefully. So, he is free to
devote his time to the serious and interesting
cases. This means that in a short time in a ward the
doctor can do a job which is technically superior
to what he could do with the same number of patients
in the Outpatient Clinic where every patient is a
new one. For all these reasons, the physicians
prefer inpatient care to clinic work.

Moreover, the routine of inpatient care gives
vivid expression to the power and status of the
doctor. Rounding a ward is very like a 'state
visit' by a high official. The doctor goes from
bed to bed in the ward; he asks each patient how he
feels, checks his chart for changes in his condition, asks the nurse for information about the

125

patient's condition and issues any orders he may
have. These are written down by the nurse who ac-
companies him. She, by her respect and subservience
emphasizes his high status and power. She stands
quietly while he speaks to the patient, speaks only
when addressed and then answers respectfully. When
the doctor jokes, she laughs. The patients, too,
hang on his every word, and they are grateful when
they are made more comfortable or cured. In short,
the rounding of the ward is a satisfying experience,
and all of the physicians at Riverton expressed a
preference for inpatient care.

In patient and outpatient care are provided
according to a schedule set in formal and informal
ways by the physicians themselves. They generally
arrive at the hospital between nine and ten o'clock
in the morning.[1] Those who are on duty in the Clinic
(four doctors each morning) round their wards
quickly and go down to the clinic. The rest round
their wards and then are finished for the day. Only
two doctors have clinic duty in the afternoon because there are far fewer patients there than in
the morning.

In generaly, the afternoons are very relaxed.
The doctors must remain in the hospital, but they
do little work. They may write discharge summaries
for patients who have been released, read journals
or relax and chat. Only when emergencies occur do
they appear in their wards. At 4:30 they are free
to leave the hospital. One physician remains on
duty to deal with emergencies, and the rest go to
their private clinics or to their homes. In effect,
most of the physicians' work in the hospital in
compressed into the hours between 9:30 in the morning and noon. This distortion of the work schedule
leads to problems in maintaining the quality of
medical care. To these we now turn our attention.

MAINTAINING THE QUALITY OF CARE

The Outpatient Clinic

In medicine, doing good work means above all
taking care to do routine tasks as well and as
fully as possible. A physician has few occasions
to do things that are dramatic but many opportunities to skimp or to neglect his duty. The quality
of outpatient care could be supervised by checking
samples of the outpatients' medical records, but
this is not done. The director has no time, and in

any case, the records of outpatients are extremely brief, and therefore checking them would probably reveal little. In short, the hospital relies mainly on the dedication and professional responsibility of its physicians to maintain the quality of care.

In theory, the professional dedication of a physician to the welfare of his patients in unlimited, but in practice few can sustain such a commitment. Consequently, the standards of professional practice come to be those that are sustained by the collegial group, and a doctor cannot easily be asked to do more than is customary. The standards that are set by Thai physicians are heavily affected by the demands of private practice, and these almost inevitably clash with those of public service. Most physicians at Riverton Hospital see patients at their private clinics from seven to eight-thirty in the morning and from five until eight or nine in the evening. Some also see patients during the noon hour. This is in addition to the very heavy patient loads which they carry at the hospital. On an average day, a physician at Riverton sees a much larger number of outpatients than a physician in group practice in the United States as the figures in Table 7.1 show. The table also shows the number of inpatients seen by each group, and here too the work load of a physician at Riverton is much heavier than that of a physician in the United States.

Clearly, it would be difficult to sustain a load as heavy as that of Riverton's doctors, and we should expect to find them making efforts to reduce it or otherwise to decrease the demands on their energies. The total number of patients in the hospital's outpatient clinic cannot be reduced because the clinic is a free, public service, and on the other hand the physicians do not wish to reduce their private patient loads. The number of patients per doctor in the outpatient clinic could be reduced if the number of doctors having outpatient clinic duty each day were increased, but that would require each physician to spend more time in the clinic, and none of them wants to do that because it would increase their overall work loads and because the work is unpleasant to them. Instead, they reduce the time spent with each patient by arriving late for work in the morning.

TABLE 7.1

COMPARISON OF WORKLOADS OF RIVERTON HOSPITAL'S PHYSICIANS
WITH WORKLOADS OF U.S. PHYSICIANS IN GROUP PRACTICE*

	Average Outpatients Per Day+	Average Inpatients Per Day#	Average Total Patients Per Day
Riverton physicians	41	30-50	71-90
U.S. physicians	25	7	32

*Figures for American physicians come from data made
available to the author by David Mechanic. For a description
of the sample on which figures are based, see Mechanic (1972:
403-405).
+The physicians at Riverton rotate clinic duty among
them so that a doctor does not see outpatients every day. This
is the number of patients seen per physician in the clinic.
#This is an estimate based on my observation at Riverton.
The wide range expresses the facts that some wards are larger
than others and that often extra beds are added to wards to
accommodate overflows of patients. Figures for numbers of
outpatients were taken from the records of the clinic at
Riverton and do not include patients seen at the physicians'
private clinics.

This strategy allows them to reduce their work
loads at the hospital and also fits the demands of
their private practices. As stated above, most of
the doctors see patients at their private clinics
in the morning before going to the hospital. It
is very difficult for a doctor to tell a patient
who arrives just before eight-thirty to go home and
return in the evening, and consequently office hours
often run beyond eight-thirty. Furthermore, physicians in some departments must round their wards
before they see patients in the clinic. So, they
may not arrive there until ten o'clock or even
later. Thus, the doctors assigned to morning
clinic duty spend at most two and a half hours
there instead of the four that they are suppose to
spend. In addition to arriving late, doctors can

limit the number of days that each must work in the clinic. At Riverton, only four physicians have clinic duty in the morning on any one day and only two in the afternoon which means that each doctor see outpatients in the clinic one morning in four and one afternoon in eight.[2]

The limitation of the time spent by the doctors in the clinic adversely affects the quality of care there. A doctor who see 41 patients in two and a half hours spends about 4 minutes with each patient. If we compare this with the time spent by group practitioners in the U.S. of about 15 minutes per patient, we can see that the Thai physician does not really have enough time to do an adequate job.

The physicians are able to limit their work in the clinic in this way in part because their power makes it difficult for the director to prevent them from doing it. In addition, their status as professionals helps them by supporting a collegial style of administration in which they set their own duty schedules. Table 6.5 showed that 73 percent of the physicians said that the assignment of duties to the doctors in their hospitals was done by staff discussion rather than by order of the director. The definition of a fair day's work is set by the staff as a group, and the director can challenge their consensus only with great difficulty. So, when we say that the physician must show commitment to detailed and careful care of his patients, this must be understood within the frame of reference established by the staff physicians, themselves. They have decided that two and a half hours in enough time to treat forty-one patients, and that is the standard adhered to.

The physicians' limitation of the time spent in the clinic has repercussions elsewhere in the hospital which force them to make still further adaptations. When the doctors spend relatively little time in the clinic, the patients must wait a long time to be seen. Those who are sophisticated know that they can reduce the wait by going to the emergency room at night for treatment instead of to the regular outpatient clinic. So, the physician on night duty sees a great many routine cases during the evening even though the emergency room is supposed to take only emergencies. A result of this is that by eleven or twelve o'clock in the evening, the doctor is very tired, and when real emergencies arise later at night he is reluctant to get up if he can avoid it.

This leads in turn to a further infraction of the rules, which is that "routine" emergency cases may be treated without having been seen by a physician at all. For example, malaria, which is still quite common in some parts of Thailand, is easy to diagnose and has a standard, routine treatment. When a patient with the typical malarial symptoms and history arrives at night, the nurse in the emergency room ordinarily telephones the physician on duty and gets permission to admit the patient and to order the appropriate treatment. The physician sees the patient only if he has some doubt of the diagnosis. The results of the survey indicate that this sort of thing is quite common in Thai hospitals. Table 7.2 shows that 76 percent of the physicians agreed that nurses treat patients at night at least sometimes.

Observation and discussion with the nurses indicate that physicians vary greatly in their willingness to allow nurses to examine, diagnose or treat patients in the doctor's stead. A very few physicians permit the nurse to examine, to diagnose, and to treat any case which she feels she can treat. Most physicians permit the nurse to examine, to diagnose, and to recommend treatment, but they reserve to themselves the power to see any cases which seem to them to be doubtful, with the exception of the kinds of minor treatments or surgery mentioned in items (4), (5), and (7) of the table. Occasionally, a physician will want to see every case himself, but such a person is usually a young doctor who wants to learn from the cases.

The reader may aky why, if nurses can examine, diagnose and treat patients under a doctor's supervision in the emergency room, they are not used in this capacity in the regular outpatient clinic. The service there would be greatly improved, and the load on the emergency room staff would be reduced. The answer is that the use of nurses in this capacity is contrary to regulations and is not yet accepted in Thai society. Nurses can treat patients informally in the emergency room at night, but they cannot be given this duty officially. (For discussions of the emerging clinical role of nurse practitioners in the United States, see Lewis and Resnick, 1967, and Silver et al. 1968).

If the emergency room nurse does not want to treat some patients herself, she can still help the doctor by making each patient wait until there are several of them and then waking the doctor to see them all at once. However, if she does that, she must face the patients and their families who can see very well that she has not yet called the doctor, and who can be quite irate and unpleasant. On the other hand, if she does not make the patients wait, she must fact the doctor who can also be unpleasant when he has been awakened unnecessarily. This dilemma is one of the most disliked parts of the nurse's role, and because of it most nurses prefer to work in the wards instead of in the emergency room, even though the work load in the wards is heavier.

Another effect of the limited staffing of the regular outpatient clinic is that the physicians sometimes use it as a screening device instead of doing thorough diagnoses. If a physician is doubtful about a case, he may admit the patient to the hospital which means, of course, that numerous patients are admitted who do not need to be hospitalized; the understaffed wards are overburdened, and the physicians' inpatient loads are increased. This is a cause of friction among the physicians, because a doctor is more likely to be unsure of the diagnosis of a case which is outside of his speciality than of a case which is in his speciality. So, when a patient is admitted unnecessarily, he is usually admitted to a ward other than that of the admitting physician. In other words, a physician can lighten his own work by shifting the load to a colleague in another department. Naturally, this is resented, but it is very difficult for the colleague to complain, because if he does it looks as though he is trying to get out of doing his job.[3] The unnecessary admission of a patient is even more likely if the person admitting him is a nurse. For, sometimes, a conscientious nurse can be assured that a doctor will see the patient only by admitting him to the hospital.

Table 7.2 also shows that the doctors are able to shift to the nurses a number of emergency treatment tasks. Nurses pump out stomachs, insert catheters, sew up wounds, open abcesses and give a number of kinds of medication. Observation indicates that these tasks are performed in the emergency room during regular clinic hours as well as during the night.

The lowering of technical standards in the clinic and the emergency room causes the doctors some discomfort. They know that, according to the standards they were taught in medical school, they

TABLE 7.2

DELEGATION OF TASKS TO NURSES

How often do nurses perform each of the following tasks in this hospital?

Tasks	Nurses Often Do It	Nurses Sometimes Do It	Nurses Never Do It	Total
(1) Give intravenous medication	86%	14%	–	100%
(2) Pump out stomachs	60	40	–	100
(3) Insert catheters	58	40	2%	100
(4) In the emergency room, sew up wounds which are not near major blood vessels	54	40	6	100
(5) Open abcesses or infected wounds which are not near major blood vessels	46	44	10	100
(6) Late at night, examine patients and treat them according to the doctor's orders given over the telephone	27	49	24	100
(7) Give analgesics that are not addictive without a physician's order	26	50	24	100
(8) Give antidote for shock when a patient has an allergic reaction to an intravenous medication	22	36	42	100
(9) Give a heart stimulant when necessary and report to the physician afterward	14	22	63	100
(10) Use a blank prescription form signed in advance by the physician to get medicine for a patient who has been admitted at night	13	29	58	100

132

TABLE 7.2 (continued)

	Nurses Often Do It	Nurses Sometimes Do It	Nurses Never Do It	Total
(11) Give blood when necessary in emergencies and report to the physician afterward	8%	28%	64%	100%

are practicing third rate medicine, but they also know that, no matter what they do, their outpatient clinic can never attain the standards of a teaching hospital. The time per outpatient might, by a considerable effort, be increased from four minutes to six, but in a teaching hospital examination and diagnosis can easily take an hour or more. So, the physicians feel that any improvement that might be made would be meaningless, and consequently they do nothing.

The Inpatients Wards

Two techniques for supervising the quality of inpatient care are used at Riverton. First, the director of the hospital rounds each ward once a week, and he checks the care of critically ill patients. If the physician incharge is present, he and the director may discuss some of the cases. The director must be very circumspect in his supervision of the doctors, however, in order to avoid offending against the canons of medical propriety. The degree of tact required of the director may be assessed from the way he presented his goals in rounding the wards to the staff physicians. They explained to me that the director had requested permission to round the wards for the purpose of checking on the condition of the wards and the quality of nursing care. No staff physician said that the director rounded for the purpose of supervising the work of the medical staff, but the director made it clear to me that this was in fact one of his purposes.

When the director encounters a case which he feels is being improperly treated, he does not ordinarily order a change in the treatment. Instead, he simply discusses the question of the treatment of the case in an academic way with the physician

in charge, who remains free to respond as he chooses
Observation indicates that the physicians are not
afraid to disagree openly with the director about
the treatment of patients.

The quality of inpatient care may also be maintained through departmental grand rounds. In grand
rounds, the entire medical staff of a department
rounds a ware together and discusses the cases. By
this means, supervision is converted into technical
discussion, and good care may be maintained without
injuring professional sensibilities. However, grand
rounds are very time consuming, and as we shall see,
time is precious to the doctors who carry heavy work
loads. As a result, grand rounds are infrequent;
the researcher observed them only once in three
months at Riverton.[4]

Nevertheless, in general the technical standards
in the inpatient wards appear to be much higher than
those in the outpatient clinic. A physician is assigned to a particular ward for a month. He has
time to order laboratory tests and to see their results,[5] to experiment with treatments and to follow
up cases. He gets a much more complete history of
each case than he would get in three minutes in the
clinic. Moreover, in a ward the physician knows his
patients well and can observe their progress. Since
he knows which cases are progressing satisfactorily
and which are still problematic, he can concentrate
his efforts where they are needed. As a result, he
can see forty patients in a ward in an hour and a
half and do a job which is technically superior to
what he could do with the same number of patients
in the clinic in twice the time.

Doing good work makes a doctor feel good because
it reinforces his positive self concept. In the
clinic, the doctors frequently mentioned to the researcher and their discouragement with the impossi-
bility of doing good work. In the wards, on the
other hand, they felt that they were successful in
upholding reasonable professional standards. Naturally, this strengthened their preference for
working in the wards and made it even more difficult for the clinic to be improved.

Another reason why the work in the wards is
superior is that the doctor-patient relationship is
personalized. In the clinic, most of the patients
are strangers to the doctor. The records of Riverton
Hospital showed that during the one month more than
half of the patients who came to the clinic before,
only a small fraction saw the same doctor they had

seen on previous visits.[6] In contrast, a ward patient who does not know who has treated him cannot
help the doctor's reputation much, but a patient
who does know the doctor's name can help or harm
his reputation greatly. So, the doctors are more
concerned to give good outpatient care.

That is not to say, however, that inpatient care
in the hospital is unaffected by the demands of
private practice. These make themselves felt in
the wards in a variety of ways. One is that many
routine tasks that are supposed to be performed by
the doctor are delegated to the nurse. Observation
indicates that, except for the surgical procedures,
the tasks listed in Table 7.2 are delegated to
nurses in wards as well as in the emergency room.

The pressures of private practice also appear
in the physicians' responses to the hospital's rule
that only the physician in charge of a ward may
treat patients there. The purpose of the rule is
to prevent the doctors from using the hospital to
treat their private patients, and it is adhered to
reasonably well during the day. During the night,
however, patients are admitted by the physician on
night duty. He cannot treat a patient in a ward
other than his own. So, when he admits someone to
another ward the physician in charge of it should
be called to reexamine the patient and prescribe for
him. However, the physician in charge does not re-
lish being called out of bed for such a reason after
his hard day's work. So, the following strategy
has been adopted; he signs several prescription
forms in blank, and these are used by the nurse in
the ward to order medication according to the directions of the physician on night duty. Thus, the
ward physician is not awakened, and the fiction
that no one but he treats patients in his ward is
maintained. Item 10 of Table 7.2 shows that this
practice is not uncommon.

Earning the Nurses' Trust

We have shown that the doctors' efforts to reduce their work loads cause them to shift tasks onto the shoulders of the nurses. In our discussion
of this practice we looked at it from the perspective of the doctors and emphasized their motives for
doing it. This cannot, however, be regarded as a
complete explanation. We must also ask why the
nurses accept the delegated tasks and what, if anything, the doctors do to earn the nurses' trust.

135

For several reasons it is not very difficult for
a doctor to earn a nurse's trust sufficiently to be
able to count on her help. First, the norms of the
hospital are well established, and when a nurse
comes into Riverton, she learns very quickly what is
expected.

I asked one of the nurses whether there was any
standing order permitting her to give intravenous
medication and to give antidote for shock in cases
of allergic reactions, and she answered that there
was no order and that she had never asked the doctors about it. She gave intravenous medication because she had seen the other nurses doing it when
she first arrived at Riverton.

Not only are there informal norms which prescribe that nurses will take over some of the doctors' work, but often the nurse must either do a job
herself or see a patient suffer for lack of immediate care. Seeing people suffer or die is always up-
setting, and for a nurse who has a professional commitment to saving lives it is particularly difficult
So, the nurse will ordinarily help if she can. Furthermore, when the nurse takes responsibility, her
autonomy is increased. Since autonomy is generally
rewarding, the nurse is motivated to accept delegated duties.

However, the nurse does not always accept delegated work. If she becomes angry at a doctor, she
may well refuse to accept some tasks. For example,
an incident occured in which a nurse used a signed
blank prescription form to order some medication for
herself. For some reason, the pharmacy refused to
honor the prescription without first calling the
doctor, and he, instead of backing up the nurse,
told the pharmacist that he could not remember having written the prescription. The nurse became very
angry and refused to write prescriptions for that
doctor for a long time thereafter. For a while he
had to go to the ward and write his prescriptions
himself. So, while the nurse is predisposed to help
the patients, and while she obtains gratification
from increased autonomy, she can withdraw into a
strict definition of her role on occasion. Therefore, the doctor must try to maintain good relations
with her, and he does so in several ways.

One thing he must do is take responsibility for
the things the nurse does in his name. If she
diagnoses a case, and the doctor tells her over the
phone to go ahead and treat it, although he has not
seen the patient, he must take responsibility.

Otherwise, if the patient were to die, the nurse would be in serious trouble. For, she would have no evidence other than her word, and perhaps her log, that he did in fact approve the treatment.

In addition to taking responsibility for treatments ordered in his name, the doctor may also help the nurse when the load gets heavy. If the number of **patients** in a ward is very large, the doctor may lend a hand and insert a catheter or administer an intravenous injection himself instead of letting the nurse do it. Responses to interview questions revealed that, when he does this, it is perceived by both sides as a favor to the nurse, and she appreciates it. This is interesting because it testifies to the existence of informal norms which prescribe that the nurse will do these things even though they are the province of the doctor. If it were not accepted that the nurse regularly did them, there would be no reason for the doctor's help to regarded as a favor.

The doctor may also help the nurse by giving a sedative to a obstreperous patient. Patients who refuse to do what the nurse asks them to do or who are extremely argumentative or critical make the nurse's work difficult for her, and when this occurs she will often ask to have the patient sedated. In this situation, the doctor can show consideration for the nurse by going to the ward without delay to do what she asks.

The doctor should also take the nurse's part in conflicts with other groups in the hospital. A hospital includes several professional groups, each with its own hierarchy and ideology. Conflicts among the groups are inevitable, especially when the work load is heavy and the resources are limited. Indeed, Strauss et al. (1963) and Bucher and Stelling (1969) have described the hospital as a "negotiated order." Negotiations among the various professional groups in the hospital occur at Riverton as they do elsewhere, and a physician can earn the nurses' gratitude by taking their side.

For example, at Riverton a conflict occured between the pharmacists and the nurses over the procedure for giving out medicines. Normally, when a physician ordered medication for a ward patient, he or a member of his family had to go to the pharmacy to pick it up. Ordinarily, it had to be paid for when it was picked up, but if the patient was too poor to pay for it, the doctor would authorize the pharmacy to give it to him free. It often happened,

however, that while the patient could afford the
medicine, he did not have enough money with him to
pay for it when he picked it up. The pharmacist
proposed that, in order to save money for the hospital, they should issue only the amount of medicine that the patient could afford to pay for in a
case of this sort, and the director issued an order
to that effect.

The nurses objected loudly because, they said,
some medicines were very expensive and were given
in large doses. A patient might lack the money for
even a single day's supply of such medication and so
might die merely because he did not have the fore-
sight to have money in his pocket. Moreover, records would have to be kept showing, for example,
that of twenty ampules of a medication that were
ordered, only twelve had been received. This would
greatly increase the ward staff's work load, the
nurses argued. The doctors sided with the nurses in
this matter and forced the director to rescind his
order. Had the doctors taken a different position,
they would likely have lost the trust of the nurses
who would thereafter have been less willing to do
extra work to help the doctors.

The doctor can also help the nurse by doing
his best to create a pleasant working atmosphere in
the ward. A doctor who takes time to chat with the
nurses, who jokes with them as they go on rounds,
who phrases his orders in a polite and gentle way,
creates a great deal of social credit for himself.
This is true anywhere, but it is especially true in
Thailand. For, in Thai society, the doctor's superior status gives him the right to maintain a great
deal of social distance between himself and the
nurses, and so, if he does not do so, he creates
gratitude on the part of the nurses, according to
Blau's (1963:215) analysis. This is partly because
the pleasant atmosphere is rewarding in itself and
partly because the willingness to tolerate intimacy
is a symbolic gesture, a pledge of willingness to
help in more concrete ways if requested to do so.

In addition to being casual and friendly, the
doctor can also take time to explain things to the
nurse and to teach her new skills. Nurses take
pride in their professional knowledge, and most of
them are glad to have opportunities to learn. The
doctor who does not care to teach the nurse who
rounds with him can save time for himself by going
quickly on rounds, giving his orders, and leaving.
If, however, he takes time to answer the nurse's
questions, he will earn her gratitude. One of the

doctors at Riverton, who was very popular with the nurses, took a great deal of time teaching a nurse the technique of reading x-rays. This was useful for the doctor because if she could depend on the nurse to read an x-ray properly, she would not have to go to the ward herself to do it but could ask the nurse for a report over the phone. However, she also earned the nurse's gratitude as was evident from the pleasure she took in rounding with this particular doctor.

A doctor may also help a nurse in more personal ways. He may make a point of attending her religious, merit-making ceremonies, of standing ready to lend her small amounts of money, or of treating her to cold drinks or meals occasionally. Finally, the doctor may simply express his appreciation of the nurse's work. Praise is unquestionably a potent reward, and the doctor who expresses his gratitude for the nurse's assistance renders her more willing to give it in the future.

Although these things are hard to measure, it does appear that the doctor receives much more from the nurse than the latter receives in return, and such was undoubtedly the opinion expressed by some nurses at Riverton.[6] This relationship illustrates well the importance of the structural and cultural variables of this study in channeling social exchange in certain directions. The doctor was able to get the nurse to take on extra work without giving an equal amount in return because the structure of the nurse's incentives already pushed her in that direction. By expanding her role, a nurse could convert a routine job into one which allowed her to exercise autonomous judgment and skill. The professional desire of the nurse to help patients in her care also pushed her to expand her role; for it was obvious that the alternative was for her to sit by and watch patients suffer or die. Therefore, most nurses were ready to take on extra responsibilities, and the doctors could obtain their help at little cost.

From this perspective it appears that the nurses were exploited by the doctors who shifted work onto the nurse's shoulders in order to be able to earn large incomes at relatively little cost to themselves. The problem with this view is that the nurses did not resist the doctors' shifting work onto them. On the contrary, they were generally glad to help, and those who did help tended to find it rewarding. For the nurses, helping was less costly

139

and more rewarding than not helping. It may well
be that this is the paradigm of exploitation, as
distinct from mere coercion: a person may be said
to exploit another when the former takes advantage
of the reward structure facing the latter to obtain
benefits without making an equitable return for
them.

Summary

This section has shown how the structural and
cultural situations of the physicians are reflected
in their behavior in treating patients. The inadequacy of their salaries leads the physicians to
engage in private medical practice. The demands of
their private practices conflict with those of their
civil service careers, but the power of the physicians and their professional autonomy allow them
to resolve the conflict by reducing the time they
spend in the outpatient clinic. This leads in turn
to a lowering of technical standards there and to
problems in other parts of the hospital. The emergency room is overloaded, patients are admitted to
the wards unnecessarily, and the ward staffs are
overburdened. The lowering of technical standards
in the outpatient department is not accompanied by
a similar decline in the inpatient department, however. It is easier for the doctors to meet their
own professional standards there, and the satisfaction obtained from doing good work reinforces the
doctors' commitment to it. Therefore, they empha-
size their work in the wards and devalue their
work in the clinic which leads in turn to further
decline in the standards of the latter. In addition, the doctors delegate numerous medical tasks
to the nurses. We saw that this can be accomplished at relatively little cost to the doctors because the nurses' incentives lead them to prefer
the enlarged responsibility to its alternatives.

The behavior of the physicians is a consequence of both structural and cultural influences,
and the data that have been presented thus far can
help us to understand better the respective effects
of each of these two sorts of factors. A structural variable, the incentive system, explains why
the physicians want to minimize the time they spend
in their hospital work, and another structural variable, power, partly explains why they are able to
accomplish this in the way that they do. The relatively powerful position of the doctor does not
provide the whole explanation, however. The pro-

fessionalism of the physician is also important for
several reasons.

First, it shields the doctor from direct supervision or criticism of his work, and second, it
justifies the staff's control over the work schedule. Professionalism is also important because
without it many more doctors would leave the civil
service altogether. Were it not for their professional desire to use and to improve their technical skills, there would be no conflict between
public service and private practice; the doctors
would simply leave the civil service and thereby
increase their incomes while decreasing their work
loads

BUILDING PERSONAL RELATIONS WITH SUPERIORS

Linguistic Usage and the Formal Display of Respect

We turn now to a discussion of personal relations between physicians and their superiors. The
most notable characteristics of these relations
from our perspective are that they are much more
egalitarian than superior-subordinate relations
among district officials and that there is less
social distance between physicians and their director than between district officials and their
district officer. This difference between the two
groups is expressed in the linguistic forms they use
respectively when speaking to superiors. Table 7.3
shows that physicians are much less likely than
district officials to use the formal, respectful
"t'an." "T'an" is a pronoun which expresses formality and social distance (like the French "vous
or the Spanish "usted") as well as hierarchical
subordination. To call someone "t'an" is to make
him both distant and superior. The professional
collegiality of physicians renders "t'an" inappropriate, but this is not to say that there is no
differentiation of status among them.

The table shows that many Thai physicians address their director as "older siblings" which is
"p'i" in Thai. "P'i expresses a combination of
respect and closeness rather than respect and distance. It expresses the fact that the director is
entitled to deference, but it also says that the
social distance between him and his staff is not
very great. Moreover, doctors do not use "p'i"
with the director alone. Any senior physician is
addressed as "p'i." Therefore, the use of this
form when speaking to the director reflects the

141

TABLE 7.3

FORMS OF ADDRESS USED WHEN SPEAKING TO IMMEDIATE SUPERIORS
(Director of District Officer)

	Older Sibling	Position Title	T'an	T'an Plus Title	Total
Physicians	51%	49%	–	–	100% (47)
District Officials	–	3	86%	11%	100% (79)

fact that his staff see him as a senior physician
to whom respect and deference are due because of his
seniority but not primarily as a bureaucratic superior.

A sizeable proportion of the doctors address
the director simply as "director." This is a title
of respect in the sense that it expresses recognition of the director's position, but it does not
express subordination. For, in Thailand titles are
often used instead of names even among equals. So,
we can see from the differences in linguistic usage
between the two groups that the relationship between the director and his staff is much closer and
more egalitarian than that between the district officer and his staff.

The relative egalitarianism of physicians appears not only in their linguistic usage but also
in their use of other sorts of social gestures.
Tables 7.4, 7.5, and 7.6 show in various ways that
physicians display less formal respect to their superiors than district officials do. The data in
Tables 7.4 - 7.6 can help us to understand another
aspect of the role of cultural factors in channeling the behavior of officials.

We have seen that physicians show their superiors much less formal respect than district officials do. This difference cannot be attributed
to power because Thai cultural norms are heavily
weighted in favor of deference to hierarchical superiors. If the cultural standards of the medical
profession were similar to those of the administrative officials, failing to address the director as
"t'an" would create unnecessary resentment on the
director's part. If the physicians were interested
in maximizing their practical freedom in a norma-

142

TABLE 7.4

VISITING THE GOVERNOR

Do you join in visiting the governor to wish him good luck
on his birthday or on New Year's Day?

	No	Yes	Total
Physicians	59%	41%	100% (49)
District Officials	26	74	100 (79)

$t = 2.91$ $df = 4$ $\alpha = .025$

TABLE 7.5

IMPORTANCE OF RECEPTIONS

In receiving visiting high officials, how important is it
that everything be arranged properly and beautifully even if
a lot of official time must be used to make the arrangements?

	Not At All Important	Not Very Important	Important	Very Important	Total
Physicians	20%	52%	24%	4%	100% (50)
District Officials	10	35	41	19	100 (79)

$t = 267.88$ $df = 4$ $\alpha = .0005$

TABLE 7.6

THE IMPORTANCE OF RESPONDING IMMEDIATELY WHEN A SUPERIOR CALLS

When the director (district officer) calls you, how important do you think it is to go in to see him immediately even if you are in the middle of a difficult piece of work?

	Not At All Important	Not Very Important	Important	Important	Total
Physicians	2%	26%	53%	19%	100% (47)
District Officials	--	3	37	60	100 (78)

$$t = 9.03 \qquad df = 4 \qquad \alpha = .0005$$

tive climate that favored extreme deference, they would avoid unnecessary conflict with superiors over matters of form by abiding by Thai standards of deference. They would address the director as "t'an," respond immediately when called, organize elaborate receptions and visit the governor on his birthday as the district officials do.[7] Since the doctors do not do so, we must conclude that the usual norms of Thai society are superseded by those of the medical profession and that the latter make possible the egalitarian style of interaction we have observed.

On the other hand, by making possible the use of egalitarian forms, professionalism leads to greater practical autonomy for the physicians. It does so because roles are only partly determined by their structural and cultural settings; in part, roles are constructed by actors. In building a role, an actor is initially constrained only by quite general norms, and it is not always clear which more specific norms are to govern the actor's behavior until he and his role partners have indicated to one another by symbolic gestures what sort of role he is to play. Forms of address and the other gestures we have discussed are among the means provided by Thai culture for an actor to indicate the sort of role he wishes to play. Once such definitions of a role have been offered and accepted, they invoke the norms that are appropriate to the role as defined. Therefore, when a physi-

144

cian addresses his superior in egalitarian ways and is not punished, it becomes difficult for the superior to demand the sorts of deference or personal services that district officers receive from their subordinates because such demands would be inappropriate among equals. Thus, the physicians exploit the available symbolic resources to build roles that are rewarding to them.

The same argument can be made with regard to the hierarchical formality used by the district officials, although they have less choice in the matter. Their use of traditional Thai forms of hierarchical deference invokes traditional Thai norms concerning superior-subordinate relations. These norms include an expectation of help and patronage from the superior which can be very useful in the subordinate's struggle for advancement.

Therefore, the data reported in Tables 7.7 and 7.8 below on the relative unwillingness of physicians, compared with district officials, to serve their superiors outside of official hours and official duties should be seen as resulting from an interaction of the structural differences with professionalism. Only further research using quantitative techniques of multivariate analysis will allow us to assess the relative importance of structural and cultural factors, but it seems clear at this point that each plays a role.

Performing Duties Unrelated to Patient Care

As mentioned above, the relative autonomy of the physician expresses itself not only in an egalitarian style of interaction but also in an unwillingness to perform services for a superior that are outside of regular, medical duties. This is shown in Tables 7.7 and 7.8.

The reader will note that while the physicians object strongly to the idea that they should be required to perform nonmedical duties, only a minority object to working outside of official hours at the demand of the director. This reflects the fact that occasions do arise when the director must ask a doctor to work extra hours. The doctors do not like to do it because it interferes with their private practices, but they accept the fact that such things cannot always be avoided. However, they give less importance to the readiness to accept such demands than district officials do.

145

TABLE 7.7

IMPORTANCE OF OVERTIME WORK NOT
COUNTING REGULAR NIGHT DUTY

How important do you think it is for you to be ready to do
your official duty as ordered by your superior outside of
official hours, not counting regular night duty?

	Not Important	Not Very Important	Important	portant	Total
Physicians	4%	31%	50%	15%	100% (48)
District Officials	1	1	51	47	100 (79)

t = 2.22   df = 4 α = .05

TABLE 7.8

ATTITUDE TOWARD PERFORMING SPECIAL
SERVICES FOR SUPERIOR

In addition to his regular duties, a physician (district
official) should be ready to serve his director (district officer) in ways outside of his regular duties as well.

	Strongly Disagree	Disagree	No Opinion	Agree	Strongly Agree	Total
Physicians	27%	41%	18%	14%	–	100% (49)
District Officials	5	22	20	39	14%	100 (79)

t = 4.73   df = 4 α = .005

146

TABLE 7.9

PATTERNS OF CONSULTATION

When you meet problems or difficulties in your
work, and you want advice, whom do you usually consult?

| | Preferred Consultant | | |
	Superior	Colleague	Total
Physicians	17%	83%	100% (47)
District Officials	75	25	100 (77)

t = 12.23   df = 4   α = .0005

Consultation

The physicians also differ from the district
officials in the use made of consultation. The
district officials consult with superiors in order
to build their trust by keeping them informed. The
physicians, on the other hand, prefer to consult
their colleagues as Table 7.8 shows. The data in
Table 7.8 reflect the different meanings that consultation has for the two groups. Observations
and interview responses indicate that physicians
consult colleagues in order to improve the care
given to patients, and to this end they choose the
best qualified consultants available.[9] District
officials, in contrast, consult their superiors
mainly to keep them informed. This difference is
consistent with our contention that physicians are
strongly motivated by the desire to do technically
good work.

CONCLUSION

In this chapter, I have shown the effects of
several structural and cultural variables on the
behavior of Thai physicians. One structural element, the inadequate incentive system, was shown
to produce the major theme in physicians' role making, namely the problem of reconciling the demands

147

of public service with those of private practice.
Physicians turned to private practice in order to
augment their incomes, but because of their professional commitment to the use of their skills,
they did not leave the civil service. Instead,
they continued to hold full time hospital staff
positions while also carrying on private practices.

The combination of these two careers produced
demands on the physicians' time that could not be
met, but, because of their very powerful position
and because of their professional autonomy, the
physicians were able to set their own work schedule
in a way which limited the demands of their hospital work and so made it possible for them to carry
on dual careers. Specifically, they reduced the
time spent in the outpatient clinic. This led to
an overload in the emergency room which the doctors
dealt with by allowing the nurses to diagnose and
treat some cases. The doctors also reduced their
work loads in the wards by delegating many routine
tasks to the nurses. These adjustments produced
a distinct lowering of technical standards in the
clinic and the emergency room. The doctors were
upset by it but felt that they could do nothing to
improve the technical standards enough to be worth
the effort. In the wards, on the other hand,
technical standards were maintained, and this
strengthened the doctors' preference for inpatient
care over outpatient care.

The delegation of tasks to the nurses involved
the doctors in social exchange with the nurses to
motivate them to accept the delegated tasks. However, we saw that the desire to serve the patients
and the preference for increased autonomy sufficiently motivated the nurses that the doctors were
able to obtain their assistance at relatively
little cost.

In building personal relations with superiors,
the doctors differed markedly from the district
officials. Where the district officials put great
emphasis on deference and a diffuse willingness to
serve their superiors, the doctors emphasized
equality, collegiality and freedom from demands
from superiors for special services. These differences appeared in several forms including the
forms of address used, the levels of willingness
to visit superiors' homes, the levels of willingness to perform special services for them, and the
patterns of consultation of the two groups.

Professionalism influenced the actions of the physicians in several ways. First, the trust accorded professional relieved the physicians of the need to have their decisions approved by superiors and so lessened the power of the latter. Second, professionalism legitimized the collegial style of administration which allowed the doctors to determine their own work schedules. Finally, professionalism made possible the use of egalitarian forms of address and other symbolic gestures which defined the roles of the doctors and their superiors in ways that made it more difficult for the superiors to demand special services from physicians.

NOTES

1. Surgeons are an exception. They often schedule surgery earlier than nine o'clock.

2. This is not strictly true, because some departments have special clinics (Antenatal Care, Cytology, and Well Baby clinics), and these take up time for some doctors. However, these clinics are held only once a week each, and only one doctor is assigned to a clinic on a given day. So, the main point that the number of physician hours in the outpatient clinic could be substantially increased remains true.

3. In principle, technical considerations could be cited in support of a complain of unnecessary admission of a patient, but to cite them would be to question the medical judgment of a colleague to his face. Medicine is not an exact science, and selection of a treatment is often a matter of medical judgement which is a polite word for informed guessing. Since the decisions of even a very good doctor often have only the most tenuous basis in data and therefore cannot be defended on technical grounds, it is considered bad form for one doctor to challenge the decisions of another. Even the director, when he wants to raise an issue concerning the treatment of a patient by a staff physician, does so by asking what his opinion is on the technical question involved, rather than by challenging the judgment of the staff physician directly.

4. In fairness to the department in which grand rounds were observed, it should be mentioned that that department holds grand rounds farily regularly according to my informants. However, the other departments rarely if ever do so.

149

5. In principle, he could order a laboratory test in the outpatient clinic, and the patient could return the following day to learn the results. In practice, the patients can hardly ever be persuaded to return. They often live in distant villages, and a visit to the clinic is extremely expensive, time consuming and boring. So laboratory tests are rarely used.

6. I know from experience as a patient that it is indeed rare to meet the same doctor twice in a Thai hospital clinic.

7. Also at Northtown Hospital. There, the nurses put up signs in various places around the hospital that read, "The nurse helps the doctor. The doctor helps the nurse." (P'ajaban chuaj mǫ. Mǫ chuaj p'ajaban)

8. Indeed, Thai people are expert at substituting deference for obedience. Siffin (1966:167) says of Thai administrators,"...the requisite response to a proposal for action always has a deference component; it does not always have a performance component."

9. The physicians are public officials and do not charge fees for consultation in the hospital. It is no favor to ask a friend to consult, and therefore friendship does not play the same important role in networks of consultation as it does in the United States. In their private practices, the doctors are almost all general practitioners and so rarely consult one another.

8. Summary and Conclusions

In the preceding chapters I have described some ways in which Thai administrative and professional activity is constrained and channeled by the situations in which it occurs. I have argued that each actor tries to organize his activities in a way which maximizes the benefits he gains from his work while minimizing its costs to him. A number of important patterns of action of Thai officials have been shown to be explainable as resulting from their attempts to obtain certain sorts of rewards under a small number of structural and cultural conditions which have been described.

Of the structural conditions the most important was the system of incentives. The inadequacy of salaries at lower levels led to strong competition for advancement among the district officials, and the diffuseness and cumbersomeness of the system of evaluation of officials' work led to a stress on two kinds of behavior in this competition. One was the emphasis on large, dramatic projects that would bring officials to the attention of their superiors, and the other was the stress on building personal relations with superiors through such means as "going in the back of the house."

The stress on large projects led in turn to the practice of raising resources locally. The latter led to social exchange with merchants and elite villagers that involved the officials in acts of varying degrees of impropriety and illegality. Moreover, the necessity of earning the trust of the merchants and elite villagers radically altered the balance of power between them and the officials.

The importance of building good personal relations with superiors was supported by data which showed that officials who were stationed close to their superiors at the provincial offices

in Northern Province were much more likely to receive double raises than those who were stationed
in outlying districts. The means used to build
personal relations included visiting the superior
at his home, doing personal services for his
family, and arranging elaborate receptions for
high officials when they visited the district.
Thus, a large number of quite different sorts of
behavior were shown to result from the structure of
incentives that faced the district officals.

The relationship between the behavior of the
district officials and their incentives became even
clearer when we compared them with those of the
physicians. The most important characteristic of
the incentive system facing the physicians was the
conflict between the desire to work in the civil
service in order to have access to hospital facilities on the one hand and the enormous profitability of private practice on the other. The doctors
reconciled this conflict by minimizing the time
spent at their work in the hospital. They accomplished this primarily by spending as little
time as possible in the outpatient clinic, and as
we saw, this practice led to a whole series of dis-
tortions in the operation of the hospital which
forced the physicians to compensate by delegating
good deal of work to the nurses. The doctors were
able to do this at relatively little cost to themselves because the nurses' incentives included the
satisfaction to be gained from increased autonomy
and from reducing the pain and suffering of the
patients.

The comparison of the physicians with the
district officials brings us to a consideration of
the second important structural variable which is
the distribution of power. The importance of
power lies in the fact that the patterns of social
exchange in any particular social situation depend
in the first instance on the way that power is
distributed. The situation of the physicians
demonstrated this in a gross way: the director of
the hospital lacked the power to coerce or to en-
tice his staff physicians to work harder in the
hospital, although officially he had the authority
to do so. He had little to offer them in exchange
for their effort, and so the level of exchange between him and them was quite minimal.

Power also affected the patterns of social
exchange in more subtle ways as the discussion of
the district officials showed. Each official had
to exploit the power he had to build his own line

of action. For example, we saw that an official
who worked in rural development who wanted to
build the trust of the villagers and thereby obtain
their consideration had to do so by expediting the
villagers' business at the district office because
that was the only way he could do it. Therefore,
the basis of his power was as much as determinant
of his own behavior as of that of the villagers.
By the same token, we have seen that the power of
subordinate officials to provide information for
their superiors led the subordinates to do so
because that was the resource they had.

However, we must remember that the individual
is more than an expression of the social structure.
It would be incorrect to say that the possession of
a certain kind of power inevitably forces its pos-
sessor to use it in a certain way. In fact, it was
only because the district officials were trying to
achieve certain ends and had to use the tools available to them that the distribution of power led them
to behave as they did. If their goals had been different, the effects of this structural variable
would also have been different.

This can be illustrated by a comparison of the
use of power made by the district officials with
that made by the physicians. In relation to their
superiors, the doctors were more powerful than the
district officials, but the doctors did not use
their power to build their superiors' trust as the
district officials did. Instead, they used it to
minimize the demands of their official positions.
In short, the possession of a certain amount or
kind of power does not, by itself, provide a sufficient explanation of an actor's behavior. The
actor's goals must also be considered.

The distribution of power also affects actors'
behavior in another way: each actor must build the
trust of those who have the power to help him.
Thus, we saw that the ability of the registration
officials to serve the public made the Local
Administration Section the hub of social exchange
at the district office. All of the development
officials had to have the trust of the Local
Administration Section in order to be able to expedite the villagers' business. Fortunately for
the heads of the other sections, the need for trust
was mutual. The deputy district officers also
needed to earn the trust of the section heads in
order to be able to call on them for assistance
with large projects. The section heads could not

easily be coerced into helping because of the
ambiguity in the distribution of power between the
district officer and the provincial section chiefs.
Therefore, the distribution of power between Local
Administration and the other sections led to several sorts of social exchange between them.

For example, the agricultural extension officer
needed the trust of the villagers in order to obtain their cooperation in improving agricultural
practices to obtain their trust, he would help to
expedite their business when they went to the district office to obtain permits or other official
documents. The agricultural extension officer could
not accomplish this by himself, however, because he
had no power to issue such papers. Therefore, to
help the villagers, he had to obtain the cooperation
of the deputy district officer in charge of registration. The latter was ordinarily glad to assist,
but in return the agriculture officer had to help
the Local Administration Section with its work when
asked to. For example, he had to help to supervise
the elections of village headmen. In general, I
argued that this sort of social exchange has emerged
among the district officials in response to their
need for flexible coordination of their work--a
need which in turn results from the national elite's
desire to maintain its position in the face of
communist and separatist insurgency.

The fact that the distribution of power limits
each actor's choice of role partners also allowed
us to trace other relationships between the resource raising patterns at the district level and
the national political structure. We said that at
the national level the political leaders traded
certain kinds of privileges, including ineffective
tax collection, to the business leaders in exchange for money for personal and political expenses. This led ultimately to the district's being starved for funds for development work, and
therefore the district officials had to engage in
social exchange with businessmen in the district.
In this exchange, the pattern found at the national
level was repeated. Widespread evasion of taxes
was condoned and other special privileges were
provided to reward businessmen for donating resources for district projects and sometimes for
personal expenses of officials. This practice was
necessary because the distribution of political
power in the kingdom made it impossible for the
central government to provide the district with
budgetary funds sufficient for its needs, and at

154

the same time the practice helped to perpetuate the deficiency that made it necessary.

The behavior of actors is also affected by cultural factors. The most important cultural factor in this study was professionalism. Professionalism is not native to Thailand, but its introduction along with Western technical training has led to great differences in attitudes and behavior between the new professionals and the more traditional Thai bureaucrats. We saw that the physicians differed from the district officials not only in having more power but also in being able to take advantage of professional norms of autonomy and collegiality in constructing their relationships with their director. Because of the norm of autonomy, physicians were trusted as professionals to make decisions regarding the care of their patients without having to obtain the director's approval.

The district officials, on the other hand, had to obtain their superiors' approval even of quite minor decisions. Since the superiors were heavily burdened with paperwork, they could not review carefully all the proposals submitted to them, and they were glad to approve recommendations from trusted subordinates without careful scrutiny. But subordinates who were not trusted found their proposals slowly and carefully checked. For this reason, district officials needed to earn their superiors' trust in order to be able to do their work. In contrast, the physicians preferred to use their professional autonomy to minimize the demands of their official positions in order to devote their time to their private practices. This difference between the two groups appeared particularly strongly in their respective patterns of consultation: the district officials preferred to consult superiors in order to keep them informed, but the physicians did not need to keep the director informed and so preferred to consult their colleagues in order to get the best possible advice.

Professionalism was also important because the professional norm of collegiality permitted the physicians to address their superiors in relatively egalitarian ways contrary to the usual norms of Thai society and of the Thai civil service. By using egalitarian forms of address, the physicians were able to invoke egalitarian norms of interaction. That is to say that when physicians addressed their superior as "director" or as "elder sibling," and he accepted it, he could not later deal with them as if he were of much higher status than they, He could not demand from them either the deference or the unquestioning obedience that bureaucratic superiors ordinarily receive from their subordinates in Thailand. Thus, by addressing the director as they did, the physicians were using a symbolic gesture to build their roles in a certain way, and this gesture was available to them because of their professionalism.

The district officials, in contrast, used the traditional bureaucratic norms of deference and obedience to superiors in building their roles. Thus, for example, the deputy district officer in charge of registration refused to make appointments with villagers in order to be able to respond immediately to a call from the district officer, even though the refusal to make appointments resulted in inconvenience for the villagers. Since the district officials usually tried hard to promote the convenience of the villagers, this showed the importance they gave to a proper display of deference. They also used traditional Thai norms of generosity to friends to build the trust of their colleagues. Officials invited each other to eat and drink and attended each other's merit making ceremonies, and by these symbolic gestures they created relationships within which favors could easily be asked and given.

These examples illustrate the general point that cultural norms function in interaction as rules for interpreting symbolic gestures. Such a rule says that a person who makes a certain geature is indicating that he wishes to enter into or to continue in a certain sort of relationship with another. Since each sort of relationship is governed by accepted norms of reciprocity, a person who indicates a desire to enter into a relationship also indicates his willingness to abide by its norms. It is for this reason that symbolic gestures can be used to build trust, and this also accounts for the feeling of betrayal we experience when a person acts as if he were a friend and then fails to live up to the obligations of a friend. Such a person is rightly regarded as a hypocrite. It should be pointed out that this sort of symbolic function is not limited to gestures that have only symbolic value. Real rewards that are exchanged between actors also have symbolic value, and offering or receiving a particular reward is evidence of the willingness to enter into a relationship in which the exchange of such rewards is appropriate.

156

It is important to note that in different cultural settings, a given gesture may have different meanings, and in building his role an actor must make use of the gestures that have the meanings he wishes to convey. Thus, for example, the bringing of small presents to official superiors in order to express loyalty, which is a common practice in Thai official circles, is appropriate because the diffuse definition of bureaucratic authority in Thailand gives to this gesture the meaning it has. In the United States, where we define official authority relations in quite a different way, such a gesture would have a different meaning and might even be seen as inappropriate. The symbolic repertory of a particular culture should be regarded as constraining the behavior of an actor, not in the sense that he must willy-nilly act out the forms of his culture, but in the sense that he must accomplish his ends by using the forms available to him. Thus, in the example referred to above, the Thai physicians did not use the traditional bureaucratic forms of deference because they had available to them another culturally defined alternative which they preferred.

By itself, the notion that a gesture may have different meanings in different cultures is by no means original, but previous theoretical formulations have provided no adequate way to link this fact with reward seeking as a basic psychological orientation. The idea of trust building used in this study allows us to integrate symbolic gestures into social exchange and hence into reward seeking. This enables us to focus on the cultural determinants of organizational behavior within the framework of the mainstream of social psychology.

I hope that this attempt to integrate cultural and structural variables with social psychological theory will help to facilitate the development of systematic, cross-cultural theory in sociology. The last few years have seen a rapid growth in cross-cultural research in our discipline, and attempts are being made by many students to conceptualize the differences among societies in terms of general variables.

The use of the comparative approach in this study has rendered its results easily comparable to results from studies in other places. Thus, for example, my finding that Thai district officials preferred to consult with superiors contrasts with Blau's (1963) finding that certain American officials preferred to consult with colleagues. A plausible explanation of this difference is that the Thai subordinate officials need to earn the trust of their superiors in a setting where rewards are given on diffuse grounds and use their control of information for this purpose. The American officials have less incentive to carry information to their superiors because they work in a setting in which statistical records of performance make the criteria for rewards relatively specific.

The behavior of the Thai officials may also be compared with that of the French officials described by Crozier (1964). He observed that it was virtually impossible for the superiors in the organizations he studied to obtain reliable information about the work of their subordinates. This may be explained by the fact that, as Crozier showed, in France rules of tenure and seniority had deprived superiors of any real power to reward subordinates who demonstrated loyalty, and therefore no one had any incentive to do so. By making possible such comparisons this study takes a small step toward a truly general comparative analysis of the effects of social structures on individual behavior.

Appendix:
The Research Methods
of This Study

One cannot assess the validity of a study's conclusions without having some notion of how the information on which they are based was gathered. Several sorts of data were collected for this study, including observations of Thai officials at work and informal interviews with them. I also obtained information from office files, from other documentary sources, and from a questionnaire survey of a sample of district officials and of provincial physicians. The observation, interviews, and documentary data provided a detailed knowledge of the attitudes and behavior of the officials who were the subjects of the study, and the survey provided quantitative support for the generalization of the findings to other officials of the same types in Thailand. I gathered data in two phases. The first phase consisted of the gathering of the various sorts of qualitative data mentioned above, and the second phase consisted of the survey.

THE QUALITATIVE PHASE OF THE RESEARCH

Data Collection

In this phase of the research, five months were spent in observation at a district office and four months at a provincial hospital. I selected the two organizations in consultation with officials of the Ministry of Health and of the Ministry of the Interior in the following way. A province was chosen that met three criteria: (1) the provincial hospital should be a large one for rural Thailand; it should have at least ten physicians, because in a very small hospital it would be difficult to disentangle the effects of structural variables from

those of the personalities of the actors. (2) The
language of the province should be Central Thai because I did not speak any other dialect. (3) The
chief administrators of both of the organizations
to be studied in the province should be willing to
permit the research to be carried out. On the
basis of these criteria I chose Northern Province[1]
as the research site. Within Northern Province, I
selected Central District Office as a site for the
study of administrators because its physical layout
(described in Chapter II) made the observation of
the work of its various sections easy.

During the period of observation at Central
District, I observed the work of and the interaction among officials both in their office and in
the field. I observed the work of all of the district's sections (except the Excise Section)[2] and
attended numerous meetings among officials and with
citizens. I asked many questions which the officials were kind enough to answer, and occasionally
I helped with the work. I examined various written
records, including reports submitted by officials
and accounts kept by the district, and with the
help of the provincial officials carried out a
survey of "double raises"[3] given in Northern Province during the preceding five years.

I interviewed the district officer, the deputy
district officers and all of the section heads as
well as the governor, the deputy governor and the
provincial clerk of Northern Province. The interviews were nondirective, were recorded on tape and
varied in length from about half an hour to about
an hour and a half, depending on the talkativeness
of the official being interviewed. They generally
ran forty-five or fifty minutes. These are rather
brief interviews for obtaining the kinds of information needed by this research, but the reader
should remember that the respondents were people
with whom I was in close contact every day for
months. The interviews were not isolated moments
during which it was necessary to gain rapport with
the respondents before serious questions could be
asked. Instead, they resembled segments of ongoing
conversations. Questions that were unanswered in
the interviews were followed up later in less formal conversations.

This is an important point. Some kinds of
questions are difficult to answer in an interview
because being a respondent in an interview puts a
person on the spot, especially if his responses are

160

being taped. His every word is recorded for pos-
terity, and he cannot deny later what he has said.
Moreover, the definition of the situation as an
interview renders him self-conscious. He is asked
deliberately to give his opinions on stated topics
or to recount his experiences in a way that can be
used for scientific research. In such a situation,
the respondent tries hard to give a coherent and
respectable view of himself, even when the reality
is neither altogether coherent nor altogether respectable. The respondent does not always succeed
in this attempt because he gets caught up in re-
counting his experiences or in giving his opinions,
and he tells more than he had intended to tell.
Nevertheless, some topics are more easily discussed
in casual conversation as they arise in the course
of ordinary business than in a formal interview.
Thus, for example, one can hardly ask an official
in an interview, "When have you used your official
position to obtain discounts on merchandise or
other favors from merchants?" Yet, such behavior
is quite common as the discussion in Chapter Four
showed, and officials are not reluctant to discuss
it if the discussion occurs naturally and does not
appear to result from the prying activity of the
researcher.

     There are also some kinds of information that
the respondent does not really know how to impart,
or the interviewer does not know how to ask for.
For example, questions about people's goals in working are likely to elicit quite sterotyped responses.
To work out a way of questioning that will get beyond these stereotyped responses to deeper levels
requires a great deal of skill on the interviewer's
part and an intimate knowledge of the respondent
and his culture. It is often easier to get such information, however, in bits and pieces in casual
conversation when people's guards are down and they
are speaking on other subjects. Therefore, the
reader should understand that the forty-five to
fifty minutes given as the average length of the
interviews refers only to the formal, taped interviews. I spent uncounted hours in conversation
with the officials of Central District in the office
itself, in the back of the district's land rover on
the way out to villages or in restaurants or food
stalls over drinks and meals.

     When I had spent about four months at Central
District, I decided that it would be useful to
observe for a short period in one or two other

districts in order to see if Central District were
typical and, if not, how it differed from other
districts. I chose two outlying districts of
Northern Province. One of these was a small, remote district, very undeveloped, and the other was
a large, well developed district similar to Central
District except that it lacked a large market center like Northtown. These two were chosen because
they appeared to provide as representative a sample
of districts as it was possible to obtain. I spent
about two weeks at the smaller district and about
one week at the larger. I interviewed formally
the district officer and some other officials of
each of the two districts.

This completed the period of research on social
exchange among district officials, and I turned my
attention to the physicians of the provincial hospital of Northtown, as had previously been agreed
with its director. However, at this point a difficulty arose. While the research at Central District was being carried out, the hospital had acquired a new director who was opposed to the research. He did not make his opposition known immediately, but instead he permitted research to be
done in the Outpatient Department only. So, I
spent month in the Outpatient Department at Northtown Hospital. I observed physicians as they examined patients and did minor surgery in the emergency room. I observed for a week on the "afternoon" (4 P.M. to midnight) shift and a week on the
"late" (midnight to 8 A.M.) shift. I attended some
meetings. From all of this a great deal of useful
information was obtained, but finally the director
told me that I would have to leave. A month was
then spent making arrangements for a new place to do
the research, and Riverton Hospital was finally
chosen.

Three months were spent at Riverton Hospital,
including about two weeks in the Outpatient Department and the remainder in the wards and operating
rooms of the Inpatient Department. I observed physicians on their rounds and nurses caring for patients as well as the interaction of doctors and
nurses during surgical operations and in the wards.
Unfortunately, I was not permitted to attend medical staff meetings. In general, working in the
hospital was more difficult and frustrating than
working at the district offices because the physicians were inclined to be suspicious of me and of
the research. I found it much more difficult

to build rapport with them than with the district officials, and with some physicians rapport was never achieved.

I collected data in the same ways at Riverton Hospital as I had at Central District except that the physicians refused to permit the taping of the interviews with them. I took copious notes, however, and as a result the interviews took about twice as long as they had at the district. Fourteen of the seventeen physicians at the hospital, including the director, were interviewed. Of the three who were not interviewed, one went abroad before she could be interviewed, and the other two made it clear that they did not wish to be interviewed. The chief of nursing was also interviewed. Formal interviews were not carried out with any of the other nurses, but I talked with them informally in the wards.

At the end of three months, I stopped collecting data at Riverton. The original schedule had called for an additional month, but it had been spent in moving from Northtown to Riverton. In order to spend more time in observation at Riverton, I would have had to reduce the time spent in the next phase of the work, and that appeared inadvisable.

Data Recording and Analysis

I kept extensive field notes of all that was observed or learned from conversation, and transcribed those portions of the interview tapes that seemed relevant or useful. The notes were classified and analyzed according to the techniques described by Lofland (1971) and by Glaser and Strauss (1967). The classification and analysis of the field and interview notes were carried on alternately with field work during the period of observation, which made it possible for me to adapt my ideas to the data as they were obtained. Thus, some of the ideas with which the study was begun turned out not to be as useful as expected and had to be reformulated. For example, I had originally conceptualized the process of exchange through which actors build their roles as a "bargaining" process. Once in the field, however, it became clear that the concept of "bargaining," unless it was used very loosely indeed, would not do as a description of the actors' behavior. So, I discarded it and in its place I adopted the notion of "social exchange" and the concept of "trust building" because they seemed to be better descriptions of the phenomena that I was observing. Thus, the theoretical explanations given in this study of behavior of the actors studied were grounded, to use Glaser and Strauss's term, in the data as they were gathered.

The analytic process through which the explanations presented in the later chapters of this study emerged may be described as a dialectical one. I went into the field with certain ideas which had come out of earlier research by me and others. I did not, as some researchers advocate, attempt to enter the field in an atheoretical frame of mind which would allow the phenomena observed to dominate the development of the study. On the contrary, I began with fairly well developed theoretical concerns. I attempted to force the data into the theoretical boxes provided by my ideas after the manner described by Kuhn (1964), and the data, not having been created with the theory in mind, resisted the attempt to make them adopt its form. When it became clear that the data could by no means be forced into a certain box it was discarded or altered.

The analysis proceeded on the assumption that its goal was to discover probable causal explanations of the behavior of Thai officials. In this study differed markedly in its approach from that recommended by Lofland (1971:89-91). He argues that qualitative analysis is not suited to research on the causes or consequences of social phenomena but should be used primarily for the description of their characteristics. That is, qualitative analysis should be as close to atheoretical as the researcher can make it. Obviously, that was not the approach taken in this research which was carried out with the intent of discovering whether the phenomena of interaction in certain types of Thai organizations would be amenable to ordering by the researcher's theoretical notions.

Because of these specific theoretical concerns, what is presented here is not a full description of the "world of the Thai official." Many of the things that officials do are not discussed or are discussed very briefly, while other things are given extended treatment. Thus, for example, routine paperwork occupies an enormous proportion of the working day of most Thai officials, and much of it is done in a routine fashion without much consideration for the need to build relations with superiors. The Thai official does not constantly think, "How can I improve my relationship with my superior?" Most of the time his attention is devoted to the quotidian, technical details of his job. However, the fact that a thing is not statistically frequent or does not occupy the front rank of importance in the consciousness of a group of people at all times does not necessarily make it unimportant in the explanation of their behavior, and conversely a great deal of time may be spent at unimportant tasks.

Therefore, what is presented in this study is a selective distortion of the world of the Thai official in which important highlights are emphasized, and other things are left invisible in the shadows. That is not to say that in my opinion the interpretation offered here would be inconsistent with the perspective of a Thai official. On the contrary, an effort has been made to present an explanation of the behavior of Thai officials in which their own stated motives supply the driving force. However, the subjects of the study would probably not organize the various parts of the picture that is painted here into a coherent whole in quite the way that I have done it. The contribution of the sociologist is to show relationships among the parts of the picture of which the actors themselves may be unaware.

THE SURVEY PHASE OF THE RESEARCH

When the qualitative phase of the research had been completed, and the data analyzed as described above, I carried out a sample survey to test the empirical generalizability of some of the findings to other Thai physicians and district officials than those whom I had observed and to compare the two groups quantitatively. A self-administered questionnaire was filled out by a sample of district officials and a sample of provincial physicians in five provinces in central and northern Thailand. This section will discuss the writing of the questionnaire, the selection of the sample, the collection of the data, and the ways in which they have been analyzed.

Writing the Questionnaire

In writing the questions, a procedure somewhat different from that usually employed by researchers

working in foreign languages was used. I was able
to avoid the cumbersome procedure of translation
and back translation because I spoke, read and
wrote Thai quite fluently. Instead, I worked with
a research assistant who was a native speaker of
Thai to write the questions directly in Thai. We
worked together on every question until we were
sure both that it meant what it was intended to
mean and that it was written according to good Thai
usage. There never was an English form of the
questionnaire, and the English forms of the questions that appear in this book were written for the
convenience of the reader.

Description of the Questionnaire

The questionnaire which the respondents filled
out provided information on background characteristics of the respondents, including such things as
age, educational attainment, type of education,
salary, seniority in the civil service, and a number of other characteristics. Then, in order to
determine whether the respondents possed the beliefs
and attitudes which had been taken as causal factors in the analysis of the qualitative data, two
kinds of questions were used.
First, there were a number of Likert-type items
like the one given below:

When the district officer calls you into his
office how important do you think it is for
you to go immediately even in you are very
busy at that moment?

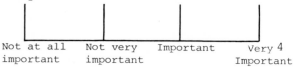

Not at all   Not very   Important   Very 4
important   important   Important

The questionnaire also included a list of eight
reasons for preferring the civil service to other
sorts of careers. These reasons had been given as
responses to unstructured questions during the first
phase of the research. Respondents to the survey
were asked to pick the three reasons which were
most important for them and to rank them in order
of importance.
In addition to the questions designed to tap
the attitudes of the respondents, there were a

166

number of questions which asked them to report the frequency with which they, or in some cases their colleagues, had engaged in certain behaviors. These questions were of the following types: first, there were some Likert-type items like this one:

> Officials who work closely with people often try to build good relations with them by expediting their work for them when they come to take care of business. Have you ever done this?

| I have done | I have | I have never |
| it often. | done it. | done it.[5] |

Some of the questions which were asked about behavior asked the respondent to choose among nominal categories of behavior, as the following one does.

> When you have problems in the work of your section, and you want advice, whom do you usually ask for advice?
>
> _____I usually ask the district officer.
> _____I usually ask my provincial superior.
> _____I usually ask a deputy district officer or the head of another section.

The form of the questionnaire received by the physicians was slightly different from that received by the district officials. The differences were of two types. First, in questions referring to relations with immediate superiors, the term "director" was used in the physicians' form while the term "district officer" was used in the district officials' form; similar differences occurred in references to colleagues. Second, in those questions which dealt with specific aspects of the work, e.g., the delegation of specific tasks to subordinates, the lists presented to the two groups were necessarily different.

The Sample

In selecting the sample for the survey, considerations of cost forced the use of cluster sampling. I chose five provinces in the central and northern regions of Thailand, and within each

167

province I surveyed the provincial hospital and the central district. I attempted to secure responses from all of the physicians in each hospital and from all of the commissioned (sanjabat) officials in each district office.

The sampling frame from which the five provinces were chosen consisted of all of the provinces of central and northern Thailand having hospitals with more than ten physicians excluding the Bangkok-Thonburi Municipality and the two hospitals in which the qualitative research had been done. There were twelve hospitals in the sampling frame, or 26 percent of the hospitals in the region. The sampling frame was limited to central and northern Thailand because the project's budget would not permit travel to other parts of the kingdom, but there is no reason to believe that the responses obtained would have been different in other parts of the country. The educated class of Thailand is a national elite. The schools in which they are educated are run according to a rigid pattern laid down by the Ministry of Education, and many people are educated in Bangkok or in parts of the country distant from their homes. Thai officials are members of a national service with strong behavioral norms and a strong sense of its own identity as an elite corps. Moreover, Thai officials are often transferred from one post to another. So, while there are differences among the regions of the country, they probably are not important in terms of the problems of interest to this study.

A more serious limitation of the sample is the fact that no responses were secured from physicians in very small hospitals. Most hospitals in Thailand have fewer than ten physicians, and one would certainly expect interaction patterns among physicians in very small hospitals to be different in some respects from those in larger hospitals. I excluded the smaller hospitals from the sampling frame because with only five hospitals in the sample I would have been unable to say anything systematic about the effects of hospital size on interaction patterns, while the inclusion of small hospitals would have greatly lowered the efficiency of data gathering. It would have been necessary to travel to a province (perhaps a very distant one) in order to collect responses from four or five physicians, and the budget would not have allowed the inclusion of a larger number of provinces to offset the smaller number of respondents per province. So, the inclusion of small hospitals would have reduced the number of physicians in the sample without leading to any substantial analytic advantage.

From the sampling frame described above, I selected five provinces randomly. In each province I collected responses from the physicians of the provincial hospital and from the commissioned officials of the district office of the central district. The questionnaires were taken to each agency in the sample and distributed to the respondents, and a week later they were collected. I attempted to secure responses from all of the physicians and commissioned district officials in each place in the sample. The actual response rate was 87 percent for the whole sample, 83 percent for the district officials and 94 percent for the physicians. There were 129 respondents in all, 79 district officials and 50 physicians.

Analysis of the Survey Responses

Statistical analyses should be adapted to the sampling procedures used and to the universe to which the researcher wishes to generalize. Typically, in sociological research the sampling frame is not the same as the population to which the researcher wishes to generalize, and this study is no exception. The sampling frame that was used certainly has no intrinsic interest, and the population that is of interest, the universe of Thai physicians and district officials, was not sampled for reasons of cost as described above. Consequently, statistical tests of significance can provide no direct test of the generality of the findings of this study. On the other hand, I have argued above that there is every reason to believe the sampling frame to be reasonably representative of the sorts of organizations sampled except for the matter of size. Therefore, significance tests were presented where they could properly be performed but they should be regarded as an indirect test of the generality of the findings only. The reader's faith in the findings must rest ultimately on other grounds than the tests.

The sample was of the dependent or "matched pairs" type. That is, provinces were chosen randomly, and in each province the hospital and the central district office were included. This lack of independence of the samples precluded many kinds of analysis. However, one can compare the means of dependent groups using the t-test for dependent

169

samples presented by Blalock (1960:179-81), and
where the data were of sorts that could appropriately be analyzed with this test, it was used. When
the data were of other sorts, percentage tables
showing the results for the sample were presented.

The use of the test for dependent samples
created a difficulty in the presentation of the
findings to the reader. The test required the
calculation of the mean for each group within pairs
(i.e., for district officials and for physicians
difference between the two means in each pair.
These differences then became the data on which the
test was performed. Since there were only five
pairs (five provinces) in the sample, there were
five differences, and the test was performed on
these five scores.

However, to present these differences in
tables in the text would not have given the reader
a clear idea of the distribution of the responses
in the sample. For that it was necessary to present percentage tables showing the responses. On
the other hand, it would have been cumbersome to
present five tables for each item in order to permit the reader to check the t-values by calculating
them for himself. I decided that the advantage of
easily comprehended tables out-weighed the advantage of being able to check the calculations; so
tables have been presented showing the responses
for the sample as a whole. The reader should
understand, however, that the t-values given cannot
be calculated from the data given in the tables but
rather must make use of scores calculated for each
province.

NOTES

1. There is no province in Thailand named
"Northern Province." This and other names given in
this study of places in which data were gathered
are pseudonyms chosen to protect the anonymity of
informants.
2. Because its work includes the suppression
of "moonshining" which is a widespread activity in
Thai villages, the excise officers are cordially
hated by the villagers. For this reason, they are
isolated at the district office and appear to have
no relations with other sections. The latter try
hard to build the good will of the villagers and
so do not wish to be seen talking to an excise officer. Even the district officer, who is the

immediate superior of the excise officer, drinks
the villagers' moonshine when they offer it, as
they frequently do.

   3. See p.   above for an explanation of
double raises.

   4. In Thai, the alternatives were "maj samk'an
loej," "maj k'ɔj samk'an," "samk'an" and "samk'an
mag."

   5. In Thai, the alternatives were "k'oej bɔj,"
"k'oej" and "maj k'oej."

References

GENERAL WORKS

Adams, J.S.
  1965   "Inequity in social exchange." Pp.
            216-99 in L. Berkowitz (ed.), Advances
            in Experimental Social Psychology,
            Vol. 2. New York: Academic Press
Blalock, Hubert M.
  1960   Social Statistics. New York: McGraw-
            Hill Book Company.
Blau, Peter M.
  1963   The Dynamics of Bureaucracy. Chicago:
            University of Chicago Press.
  1964   Exchange and Power in Social Life.
            New York: John Wiley and Sons.
Blauner, Robert
  1964   Alienation and Freedom. Chicago: Uni-
            versity of Chicago Press
Bryant, John
  1969   Health and the Developing World.
            Ithaca: Cornell University Press.

Bucher, Rue and Joan Stelling
  1969   "Characteristics of professional or-
            ganizations." Journal of Health and
            Social Behavior 10:3-15.
Burns, Tom and G. M. Stalker
  1961   The Management of Innovation. London:
            Tavistock Publications.
Chinoy, Ely
  1955   Automobile Workers and the American
            Dream. New York: Doubleday and Company
Cole, Robert E.
  1971   Japanese Blue Collar. Berkeley: Uni-
            versity of California Press.

Coser, Lewis
    1956   The Functions of Social Conflict. New
              York: The Free Press.
Coser, Rose Laub
    1963   "Alienation and social structure."
              Pp. 231-61 in Eliot Freidson (ed.),
              The Hospital in Modern Society. New
              York: The Free Press of Glencoe.
Crozier, Michel
    1964   The Bureaucratic Phenomenon. Chicago:
              University of Chicago Press
Cyert, Richard and James G. March
    1963   A Behavioral Theory of the Firm. En-
              glewood Cliffs, N.J.: Prentice-Hall.
Dalton, Melville
    1959   Men who Manage. New York: John Wiley
              and Sons, Inc.
Emerson, Richard M.
    1962   "Power-dependence relations." American
              Sociological Review 27:31-40,
Glaser, Barney G. and Anselm L. Strauss
    1967   The Discovery of Grounded Theory.
              Chicago: Aldine Publishing Company.
Glaser, William A.
    1963   "American and foreign hospitals: some
              sociological comparisons." Pp. 37-72
              in Eliot Freidson (ed.), The Hospital
              in Modern Society. New York: The Free
              Press of Glencoe.
Goffman, Erving
    1961   Asylums: Essays on the Social Situa-
              tion of Mental Patients and Other In-
              mates. Garden City, N.Y.: Doubleday
              and Co.
Goldner, Fred H. and R. R. Ritti
    1967   "Professionalization as career immo-
              bility." American Journal of Sociology
              72:489-502.
Goss, Mary E. W.
    1963   "Patterns of bureaucracy among hospi-
              tal staff positions." Pp. 170-93 in
              Eliot Freidson (ed.), The Hospital in
              Modern Society. New York: The Free
              Press of Glencoe.
Gouldner, Alvin W.
    1957   "Cosmopolitans and locals: toward an
              analysis of latent social roles." Ad-
              ministrative Science Quarterly 2:281-
              92.

Hall, Richard H.
    1962   "Intra-organizational structural vari-
              ations: Application of the bureaucratic
              model." Administrative Science Quarter-
              ly, 7:295-308.
    1968   "Professionalization and bureaucratiza-
              tion." American Sociological Review 33:
              92-104.
    1972   Organizations, Structure and Process.
              Englewood Cliffs, New Jersey: Prentice-
              Hall, Inc.
Hastorf, Albert H., David J. Schneider and Judity
Polefka
    1970   Person Perception. Reading, Mass: Addi-
              son-Wesley Publishing Company.
Hickson, D.J., C. R. Hinings, C.A. Lee, R.E. Schneck
and J.M. Pennings
    1971   "A strategic contingencies theory of
              intra-organizational power." Admini-
              strative Science Quarterly 16:216-29.
Homans, George Caspar
    1961   Social Behavior: Its Elementary Forms.
              New York: Harcourt, Brace and World.
Hovland, Carl I., O.J. Harvey and Muzafer Sherif
    1957   "Assimilation and contrast effects in
              reaction to communication and attitude
              change." Journal of Abnormal and Social
              Psychology 55:242-252.
Jones, E.E.
    1964   Ingratiation: A Social Psychological
              Analysis. New York: Appleton-Century-
              Crofts.
Kruglanski, Arie
    1970   "Attributing trustworthiness in super-
              visor-worker relations." Journal of
              Experimental Social Psychology 6:214-32.
Kelly, H. H.
    1967   "Attribution theory in social psycho-
              logy." Nebraska Symposium on Motiva-
              tion in 15:192-138.
Kuhn, Thomas S.
    1964   The Structure of Scientific Revolutions.
              Chicago: The University of Chicago Press
Lawrence, Paul and Gary Lorsch
    1967   Organization and Environment. Cambridge.
              Harvard University Press.

Lewis, Charles and Barbara Resnick
    1967   "Nurse clinics and progressive ambu-
            latory patient care." New England
            Journal of Medicine 227: 1236-41.
Lewis, Oscar and Victor Barnouw
    1967   "Caste and the jajmani system in a
            north Indian village." Pp. 110-134 in
            Jack M. Potter, May N. Diaz and George
            M. Foster (eds.), Peasant Society,
            Boston: Little, Brown and Company.
Lofland, John
    1969   Deviance and Identity. Englewood
            Cliffs, N.J.: Prentice-Hall, Inc.
    1971   Analyzing Social Settings. Belmont,
            California: Wadsworth Publishing Com-
            pany, Inc.
March, James G. and Herbert A. Simon
    1958   Organizations. New York: John Wiley
            and Sons.
Marsh, Robert M. and Hiroshi Mannari
    1971   "Lifetime commitment in Japan: roles,
            norms and values." American Journal
            of Sociology 76:795-812.
Mechanic, David
    1962   "Sources of power of lower partici-
            pants in complex organizations." Ad-
            ministrative Science Quarterly 7:349-
            64.
    1972   "General medical practice: some com-
            parisons between the work of primary
            care physicians in the United States,
            England and Wales." Medical Care 10:
            402-20.
Miller, George A.
    1967   "Professionals in bureaucracy: aliena-
            tion among industrial scientists and
            engineers." American Sociological
            Review 32:755-67.
Myrdal, Gunnar
    1968   Asian Drama (3 vols.). New York:
            Random House.
Perrow, Charles
    1961   "The analysis of goals in complex or-
            ganizations." American Sociological
            Review 26:854-66.
    1964   "Hospitals, technology, structure and
            goals." Pp. 910-71 in James G. March
            (ed.), The Handbook of Organizations.
            Chicago: Rand McNally and Co.

Powell, John Duncan
　1970　"Peasant Society and Clientelist
　　　　Politics." American Political Science
　　　　Review, 64:411-425.
Scott, James C.
　1972a　Comparative Political Corruption. En-
　　　　glewood Cliffs, N.J.: Prentice-Hall,
　　　　Inc.
　1972b　"Patron-Client Politics and Political
　　　　change in Southeast Asia." American
　　　　Political Science Review, 66:91-113.
Scott, Robert A.
　1976　"Deviance, sanctions, and social inte-
　　　　gration in small-scale societies."
　　　　Social Forces 54:604-20.
Silver, Henry K., Loretta C. Ford and Lewis R. Day
　1968　"The pediatric nurse-practitioner pro-
　　　　gram." Journal of the American Medi-
　　　　cal Association 204:298-302.
Strauss, Anselm
　1962　"Transformations of identity," Pp. 63-
　　　　85 in Arnold M. Rose (ed.), Human Be-
　　　　havior and Social Processes. Boston:
　　　　Houghton Mifflin Company.
Strauss, Anselm, Leonard Schatzman, Dannta Ehrlich,
Rue Bucher and Melvin Sabshin
　1963　"The hospital and its negotiated or-
　　　　der." Pp. 147-69 in Elio Freidson
　　　　(ed.), The Hospital in Modern Society.
　　　　New York: The Free Press of Glencoe.
Taub, Richard P.
　1969　Bureaucrats Under Stress. Berkeley:
　　　　University of California Press.
Thibaut, J. W. and H. H. Kelly
　1959　The Social Psychology of Groups. New
　　　　York: John Wiley and Sons.
Thompson, James D.
　1967　Organizations in Action. New York:
　　　　McGraw-Hill Book Company.
Walster, Elaine, Ellen Berscheid and G. William
Walster
　1973　"New directions in equity research."
　　　　Journal of Experimental Social Psy-
　　　　chology 25:151-76.
Wilensky, Harold L.
　1956　Intellectuals in Labor Unions.Glencoe:
　　　　The Free Press.

WORKS ON THAILAND

Works in English

Blaug, Mark
    1971   "A post mortem of manpower forecasts
             in Thailand." Journal of Development
             Studies 8:59-78.
Bryant, John D.
    1969   Health in the Developing World. Ithaca
             Corness University Press.

Dieter-Evans, Hans
    1966   "The formation of a social class
             structure: Urvanization, bureaucrati-
             zation and social mobility in Thai-
             land." Journal of Southeast Asian
             History, 7:100-115.
    1969   Loosely Structured Social Systems:
             Thailand in Comparative Perspective.
             Cultural Report Series No. 17, Yale
             University Southeast Asia Studies.
             New Haven: Yale University Southeast
             Asia Studies.
Hanks, Lucien, Jr. and Herbert P. Phillips
    1961   "A young Thai from the countryside."
             Pp. 637-56 in Bert Kaplan (ed.),
             Studying Personality Cross Culturally.
             Evanston, Illinois: Row, Peterson, and
             Company.
Horrigan, Frederick James
    1959   "Local government and administration
             in Thailand." Unpublished Ph.D. dis-
             sertation, Indiana University.
Ingram, James C.
    1971   Economic Change in Thailand 1850-1970.
             Stanford: Stanford University Press
Lewchalermwong, Anan
    1972   Taxation and Tax Reform in Thailand.
             Bangkok: Kurusapha Ladprao Press.
Maxwell, William Edgar
    1975   "Modernization and mobility in patri-
             monial medical elite in Thailand."
             American Journal of Sociology 81:465-
             90.
Meksawan, Arsa
    1961   "The role of the provincial governor
             in Thailand.' Unpublished Ph.D. dis-
             sertation, Indiana University.

Moerman, Michael
    1968   Agricultural Change and Peasant Choice
                in a Thai Village. Berkeley: Univer-
                sity of California Press.

    1969   "The Thai village headman as synaptic
                leader." Journal of Asian Studies,
                28:535-49.

Neher, Clark
    1969   "District level politics in northern
                Thailand." Unpublished Ph.D. disser-
                tation, University of California at
                Los Angeles.
    1972   "The politics of change in rural Thai-
                land. Comparative Politics 4:201-16.
NIDA
    1972   Seventh Annual Report of the National
                Institute of Development Administra-
                tion. Bangkok: Administration of the
                State Universities Bureau.
Nivat, Prince Dhani
    1976   "The old siamese conception of the
                monarchy." Pp. 25-38 in Clark D.
                Neher (ed.), Modern Thai Politics.
                Cambridge, Mass: Schenkman Publishing
                Company.
Phillips, Herbert P.
    1967   "Social contact vs. Social Promise in
                a Siamese Village. Pp. 346-67 in Jack
                M. Potter, May N. Diaz and George M.
                Foster (eds.), Peasant Society. Boston:
                Little, Brown and Company
    1970   Thai Peasant Personality. Berkeley:
                University of California Press.
Piker, Steven
    1968   "Sources of stability and instability
                in rural Thai society." Journal of
                Asian Studies 27:777-90.
Potter, Jack M.
    1976   Thai Peasant Social Structure. Chicago:
                University of Chicago Press.
Rabibhadana, Akin
    1969   The Organization of Thai Society in the
                Early Bangkok Period. Data Paper Num-
                ber 74, Southeast Asia Program. Cor-
                nell Southeast Asia Program
Riggs, Fred W.
    1966   Thailand: The Modernization of a Bu-
                reaucratic Polity. Honolulu: East-West
                Center Press.

Romm, Jeff
    n.d.   "Urbanization in Thailand" Interna-
            tional Urbanization Survey, The Ford
            Foundation
Roth, David F.
    1976   "Dimensions of policy change: towards
            an explanation of rural change poli-
            cies in Thailand." Asian Survey, 16:
            1043-1063.
Rubin, Herbert J.
    1973   "Will and awe: illustration of Thai
            villager dependency upon officials."
            Journal of Asian Studies 32:425-44.
    1974   Modes of bureaucratic communications:
            examples from local Thai Administra-
            tion. Sociological Quarterly, 15:212-
            230.
Samudavanija, Chai Anan
    1971   "The politics and administration of
            the Thai budgetary process." Un-
            published Ph.D. dissertation. Univer-
            sity of Wisconsin.
Scoville, Orlin J. and James J. Dalton
    1974   "Rural Development in Thailand: the
            ARD program." Journal of Developing
            Areas, 9:53-58.
Shor, Edgar L.
    1962   "The public service." Pp. 23-40 in
            Joseph L. Sutton (ed.), Problems of
            Politics and Administration in Thai-
            land. Bloomington: Institute of
            Training for public service.
Siffin, William J.
    1966   The Thai Bureaucracy. Honolulu: East-
            West Center Press.
Thirabutana, Prayuab
    1971   Little Things. London: Fontana Collins.
Vella, Walter F.
    1955   The Impact of the West of Government
            in Thailand. (University of Califor-
            nia Publications in Political Science,
            Vol. 4, No. 3) Berkeley: University
            of California Press.
Wales, H. G. Quaritch
    1965   Ancient Siamese Government and Admini-
            stration. New York: Paragon Book Re-
            print Corp.

Wichaidit, Thawat
    1973   "Provincial administration in Thai-
             land: its development and present
             problems." Unpublished Ph.D. disserta-
             tion, University of Wisconsin.
Wilson, David A.
    1962   Politics in Thailand. Ithaca: Cornell
             University Press.
Wyatt, David K.
    1976   "Family politics in nineteenth cen-
             tury Thailand," Pp. 54-72 in Clark D.
             Neher (ed.), Modern Thai Politics,
             Cambridge, Mass.: Schenkman Publishing
             Company

Works in Thai

Krom Wichakan, Krasuang Sᵾksatikan
    1970   Baebrian Sangkomsᵾksa Wicha Sint'am
             Prajok Mat'ajomsᵾksa Tǫnplaj. Bangkok:
             Kurusapha Ladprao Press.

Sawasdi, Woratheb and Nivat Wachiraworakara
    1973   "Sangk'om t'ai mi k'rongsang t'i luam
             Ǧing rᵾ." The Thai Journal of De-
             velopment Administration 13:464-77.
Suwannabul, Isara
    1971   "Nakbǫrihan suan p'umip'ak: kansᵾksa
             chap'ǫ kǫrani k'arachakan Ǧangwat
             pranak'ǫn si ajut'aja." Pp. 77-101
             in Wǫřasan Sangk'omsat, Chabab p'iset
             rajngan bᵾangton KanwiǦaj Ajut'aja.
             Bangkok: Chulalongkorn University
             Social Science Research Institute.